HOW TO SURVIVE
ARMAGEDDON

JOHN C. BRUNT

REVIEW AND HERALD® PUBLISHING ASSOCIATION
Since 1861 | www.reviewandherald.com

Published by Review and Herald® Publishing Association, Hagerstown, MD
21741-1119

Review and Herald® titles may be purchased in bulk for educational, business,
fund-raising, or sales promotional use. For information, e-mail SpecialMarkets@
reviewandherald.com

The Review and Herald® Publishing Association publishes biblically based materials
for spiritual, physical, and mental growth and Christian discipleship.

The author assumes full responsibility for the accuracy of all facts and quotations as
cited in this book.

Unless otherwise indicated, Scripture quotations are from the *Holy Bible, New
International Version.* Copyright © 1973, 1978, 1984, 2011 by Biblica, Inc. Used by
permission. All rights reserved.

This book was
Edited by Gerald Wheeler
Copyedited by Judy Blodgett
Designed by David Berthiaume
Cover art by istockphoto.com
Typeset: Bembo 11/13

PRINTED IN U.S.A.

15   14   13   12   11   5   4   3   2   1

Library of Congress Cataloging-in-Publication Data

Brunt, John, 1943-   .
  How to survive Armageddon / John C. Brunt.
     p. cm.
1. Armageddon. 2. End of the world. I. Title.
  BT877.B78 2011
  236'.9—dc22

                                                2011014155

ISBN 978-0-8280-2582-9

This book is dedicated to the wonderful, committed, gifted pastoral colleagues with whom I have had the privilege of ministering at the Azure Hills church over the past decade.

For we are coworkers in God's Service (1 Corinthians 3:9)

Darren Carrington
John Choi
Salim Elias
Marlene Ferreras
Alex Harter
Mark Holm
Carmen Ibañez
Roy Ice
Alger Keough
Michael Knecht
Maria Lee
Dante Marruffo
Andy McRae
Mike Porter
Samir Selmanovic
Lamar Sandiford
Jared Wright

CONTENTS

Chapter 1

UPSIDE DOWN

A couple years ago I spent a few days in New York City. As I walked the crowded streets, people constantly handed me things. Most were advertisements of some sort for all kinds of different products. But second on the list were pamphlets about the end of the world. Lots of would-be prophets seem to be talking and thinking about what will happen then, and apparently quite a few have written down their thoughts to try to convince the rest of us.

For example, in Times Square a woman handed me two pamphlets about the end of the world and the events of the last days. One was all about the number 666. It charged that right now our government, along with those of other nations, is trying to create a cashless society by making a computer chip that it will seek to implant in all of us. The chip is the mark of the beast, and all who receive it will go to hell. According to the pamphlet it is vitally necessary that we understand the details of the conspiracy or we will be fooled into accepting it.

The second pamphlet was all about what some call the rapture. It presented the view that soon there will be a day on which all of God's people will simply disappear from the earth. God will snatch them up to heaven, but the rest of the world will go on functioning as before. However, a time of terrible tribulation will break out soon afterward and will last for seven years; then Jesus will return to the earth.

From Times Square I walked down 42nd Street to Grand Central Station. There someone handed me still another pamphlet. It argued that when Jesus said that no one would know the day or hour of His coming (Matthew 24:36), that was true only until 1988. At that date God began revealing the exact time of His return to true believers. If you were going to be ready for that day, you would need to know the outline of the final events presented in the tract—or so the authors claimed.

I don't have to travel to New York, however, to be deluged with material about scenarios of last-day events and the end of the world. A few weeks ago, outside my own church in Grand Terrace, California, someone handed me a DVD and told me that I needed to watch it. I played some of it, but not the whole four hours. It said that the close of probation, in preparation for the second coming of Jesus Christ, had begun on September 11, 2001, when terrorists destroyed the World Trade Center in New York. Again, the speaker on it urged that in order to be prepared for the end of the world and be saved, I must know about the events that it portrayed in detail.

End-time scenarios seem to pop up everywhere. I walked into my supermarket and found a big display of books for sale that tell about last-day events. What is a person to do? Is it really important to know about how the world is going to end, or even to think about such things? Why not just go on living each day and not worry about the future of the world?

At one time many people simply believed that

earth's history would go on forever. One of the leading New Testament theologians of the twentieth century, writing about 80 years ago, labeled the picture of the return of Jesus given in the New Testament a myth. He said the New Testament eschatology (that word means the study of last things and the end of the world) never took place as the writers expected, and now we know that it never will.

"We can no longer look for the return of the Son of Man on the clouds of heaven or hope that the faithful will meet him in the air. . . .

"It is impossible to use electric light and the wireless and to avail ourselves of modern medical and surgical discoveries, and at the same time to believe in the New Testament world of spirits and miracles. . . .

"The mythical eschatology is untenable for the simple reason that the parousia [coming] of Christ never took place as the New Testament expected. History did not come to an end, and, as every schoolboy knows, it will continue to run its course."[*]

Today, however, not every schoolboy knows that history will continue to run its course. Scientists and political leaders seriously consider how our world will end. Some scientists worry that global warming could bring human history to an end. Others are concerned that we might eventually suffocate in a sea of polluted air. Political scientists consider the possibility that we might destroy human life through nuclear war. Somehow the view that everyone knows the world will just keep going on forever is losing its popularity. This in itself may be a sign that God is preparing the earth for its grand climax.

Of course, people still make fun of the idea of the

How to Survive Armageddon

end of the world. Cartoons mock would-be prophets who carry signs announcing its impending doom. I recently saw a satirical video that spoofed the debates about evolution and creation being taught in public schools. In this mock debate scientists and theologians argued about whether children should be taught the scientific or religious view of the end of the world in their public schools. The scientists wanted to instruct children that the world would end in the heat of global warming. The religious types sought to warn students that the world would perish in the fires of Armageddon. Not a terrific choice!

Is it possible that behind the satire and mocking is genuine fear about what will eventually happen to our world? Could it be that the various scenarios appearing in books, pamphlets, and DVDs actually grow out of something deep in the minds of lots of people?

If so, that still raises the dilemma of which account to listen to. They all seem to be different, and they all claim to be the right one. So whom do you believe? It's tempting to throw your hands in the air and forget them all.

I personally have some discomfort with most end-time scenarios. First, all of them seem to say that you have to know and understand *their* ordering of events if you are going to be prepared for the end of the world. For many Christian scenarios it means figuring out just how the tribulation, plagues, the giving of the mark of the beast, the emergence of the antichrist, the close of probation, and a number of other events all fit together. But the proposed sequences with their often contradictory outlines can't all be right.

A second problem I have with them is the general

sense of fear and foreboding they share. The spirit is one of constant nail-biting. And it's true not only of pessimistic secular people who worry about pollution and nuclear war. Many religious people fear the end, because they see it in the outworking of a harsh and vengeful God.

Third, so many of the scenarios try to figure out prophetic dates and times in an attempt to decipher the future and date the end of time. Perhaps the whole endeavor of charting all the events that will lead up to the end of the world is a misguided effort. Instead, I want to turn the whole subject of last-day events upside down. I believe there is good news about the end of the world. Furthermore, while I feel that we can know what is coming in the future, I have concluded that most of the end-time scenarios you read about in pamphlets have missed the point.

You see, the Bible presents the story of Jesus, and this story includes not only what Jesus did while He was here on earth—it also abounds with promises He made about the future as well. In the next chapter we look at one of those promises. It will show us the most vital piece of information that we need to know about the future and the end of the world. This one bit of information takes away the fear and replaces it with joy and hope. And it challenges the whole idea of most of the end-time charts and scenarios that confront us in the streets, on the DVDs, and even in many churches.

Let's move on to chapter 2 and see what this good news is all about.

---

* Rudolf Bultmann, "New Testament and Mythology," in *Kerygma and Myth*, ed. Hans Werner Bartsch (New York: Harper and Row, 1961), pp. 3, 4.

CHAPTER 2
THIS SAME JESUS

The book of Acts is the fifth book of the New Testament and the second volume of two written by Luke, a companion of the apostle Paul. In his first book, the Gospel of Luke, he tells the story of Jesus' birth, ministry, death, and resurrection. Then in the second he shows how the Holy Spirit led Jesus' followers to take the good news recorded in the first book throughout the world to form the Christian church. One of the great promises of the Bible comes in the first chapter of Acts in which Luke records how Jesus and His disciples met together 40 days after His resurrection.

"Then they gathered around him and asked him, 'Lord, are you at this time going to restore the kingdom to Israel?' He said to them: 'It is not for you to know the times or dates the Father has set by his own authority. But you will receive power when the Holy Spirit comes on you; and you will be my witnesses in Jerusalem, and in all Judea and Samaria, and to the ends of the earth.' After he said this, he was taken up before their very eyes, and a cloud hid him from their sight. They were looking intently up into the sky as he was going, when suddenly two men dressed in white stood beside them. 'Men of Galilee,' they said, 'why do you stand here looking into the sky? This same Jesus, who has been taken from you into heaven, will come back in the same way you have seen him go into heaven'" (Acts 1:6-11).

Jesus' disciples were excited. They had been expecting Him to set up a kingdom on earth, and they thought now would be the perfect time. So they asked Him if it was. They wanted to know *when* Jesus was going to establish His earthly kingdom. But if it wasn't now, when would it be? And *what* was going to happen next?

Jesus instead redirected their focus. He told them it wasn't for them to know the dates and times and events. God the Father would take care of that. Nor was it their job to decipher end-time dates and events. Rather, they were to be witnesses to what Jesus had done and carry the message from where they were at the time, the city of Jerusalem, to the areas around them, Judea and Samaria, and then on to the ends of the earth. Thus their responsibility wasn't to *know* all about the timing of Jesus' kingdom, but to *go* and be witnesses for Jesus to prepare people for its coming.

After Jesus made this clear, He disappeared from their sight into a cloud. Then two men, presumably angels or messengers of God, came to them and asked them why they were gazing up into the sky. They promised the disciples that Jesus would return in the same way they saw Him leave. As we will see throughout this book, it is this promise (and many others like it in the New Testament) that gives Christians hope for the future. We believe the future of our world is in the hands of this same Jesus whose story the Gospels, the first four books of the New Testament, so dramatically tell us.

And we consider this to be particularly good news, for the Jesus we find in the Gospels is someone who can be loved and trusted. He is the one who is coming again and holds our world's future in His hands. We prepare ourselves for the end of earth's history not by knowing *events,* but by knowing *Jesus.*

Who is this Jesus? Why can we trust Him? Think about the following.

The promise the two divine messengers gave the disciples means that the Jesus who is coming back is the same being who was willing to leave the glories of heaven to be born in a barn with smelly animals just because He loves us so much. In a beautiful hymn about Jesus in Philippians 2:6, 7, Paul says that Jesus was the one:

> "Who, being in very nature God,
>   did not consider equality with God
>   something to be used to his own advantage;
>   rather, he made himself nothing
>   by taking the very nature of a servant,
>   being made in human likeness."

The Jesus who was in very nature God, but came to this world to become human and save us, is coming again—and that is good news.

The promise in Acts 1 declares that the one who is returning to this earth and holds the future of our world in His hands is the same Jesus confronted by angry accusers who had caught a woman in the act of adultery. They were about to stone her, but Jesus sent them running. Then He asked her where her accusers were. When she acknowledged that they had disappeared, Jesus told her, "I don't condemn you either. Go and sin no more" (see John 8:11).

This same Jesus, a Jesus of compassion and for-giveness, is coming again—and that is good news.

The promise in Acts 1 assures us that the one who will meet us at the end of history is the one who liked people so much that He went to their parties and was accused of hanging out with the wrong kind of peo-ple. He performed His very first miracle at a wedding reception. Jesus welcomed all people, whether they were from high society or poor beggars.

This same Jesus, the people lover, is coming again—and that is good news.

The promise of Acts 1 also reminds us that the fu-ture of our world and of our lives rests in the hands of one who could stand and weep at the death of His best friend, Lazarus. But He could also say the word and have Lazarus come forth from the tomb, alive and well, after four days (John 11).

This same Jesus is coming again—and that is good news.

The promise of Acts 1 comforts us with the fact that the one who is coming back to our world is the same one who was willing to go to the worst instrument of torture that His culture knew, the cross, and suffer there even though He had the power to step down and avoid it all—again because He loves us so much. Paul continues the hymn from which we quoted earlier in Philippians 2:8:

> "And being found in appearance as a man,
> he humbled himself by becoming
> obedient to death—
> even death on a cross!"

This same Jesus, the Jesus of the cross, is coming again—and that is good news.

How to Survive Armageddon

As Jesus suffered torture on that cross, He looked down on the very people who spat on Him and mocked Him, who beat Him and forced a crown of thorns on His head, and He prayed, "Father, forgive them, for they do not know what they are doing" (Luke 23:34).

This same forgiving Jesus is coming again—and that is good news.

Finally, when they took Jesus from the cross and placed Him in a tomb, that tomb was not able to hold Him. In spite of a large stone, powerful soldiers, and Satan himself, Jesus burst out of the tomb as the resurrection and the life.

This same living, life-giving Jesus is coming again—and that is good news.

If you have not done so before, I encourage you to take one of the four Gospels at the beginning of the New Testament and read it through. See who this Jesus is. Contemplate what He has done for us. Get a clear picture of His character of love. Then think about what it would mean to have your future in His hands. Consider what it would be like to know that He is the one who holds not only your future but also that of the world. Reflect upon what good news that would be.

The promise of the second coming of Jesus can become the hope that God intends it to be only when we know who "this same Jesus" is who is returning to our world to save us and bring an end to sin and death.

We become prepared for His arrival, not by knowing what events will take place, but by knowing Jesus and trusting Him as our Savior who will rescue us from sin and death and give us eternal life. Most of the end-time scenarios have it all wrong. They emphasize figuring out when Jesus will show up and how current events may help us decipher times and dates, the very things Jesus told His disciples were not for them to know (as we will see in subsequent chapters). Instead, He summons us to know Him.

On the other hand, Jesus did warn that before His return false prophets and false messiahs would appear and that Satan would use them to try to deceive God's people (see Matthew 24). Therefore it is important to understand what Jesus tells us about His return. The focus is on knowing Him, but He does give us warnings to keep us from being taken in by false, speculative scenarios. So it is important to see what the New Testament teaches about the return of Christ and how it will occur, and that is what we will do throughout this book.

But we must never take our focus off the most important point of all—Jesus is coming again, and we prepare for that day by knowing Him so well that none of Satan's deceptions could make us fall for a counterfeit.

Today many people worry about what monsters lurk ahead at the end of our earth's history. They tremble before threats of nuclear destruction, global warming, a suffocating sea of smog, or even an angry, vengeful God. But for Christians the end is good news, because it is this same Jesus, the one whom we come to know and love in the Gospels, who shelters our future in His hands.

Recently I was with two of my three grandsons, a 2½-year-old and a 5½-year-old. They made my day when they brought a stack of books, climbed up on my lap (one on each knee), and announced, "Read to us, Grandpa." The younger one handed me a book and said, "Read this one first!"

It was a book about one of the characters from Sesame Street, Grover. The book, by Jon Stone and Michael Smollin, is titled *The Monster at the End of This Book Starring Lovable, Furry Old Grover.*[*] When I started reading the book, we learned that Grover is deathly afraid of monsters, and that there was a monster at the end of the book. Therefore Grover begged, pleaded, admonished, and implored the reader not to turn the pages of the book. He didn't want to get to the monster.

I asked at the end of the first page, "Should we turn the page? Grover doesn't want us to." And my grandsons said, "Turn the page!" When we did, Grover was panicked, and he begged us not to go to the next page, but the boys told me to keep reading. As the story continued Grover became more agitated and more insistent. "You don't know what you're doing to me. Don't turn another page!" But the boys insisted, "Turn the page!"

Finally we got to the end of the book and found that there was no monster—just lovable, furry old Grover. And the boys laughed.

Many worry about the monsters that lurk at the end of the book as we turn the pages of our world's history. But the Bible tells us not to fear. There is no monster of nuclear destruction or natural catastrophe at the end of the book. There is instead *this same Jesus*—and that is good news.

---

[*] Big Little Golden Books, 2004.

CHAPTER 3
HOW CAN THE LAST DAYS
LAST SO LONG?

If you were going to make a chart of the events of the end time, where would you begin? What are the first "last-day events"? Well, I wondered about this, so I searched the Web for charts about end-time events. I looked at quite a few examples and found that many of them begin last-day events as far back as 200 years.

That seems like a long time ago. I work with a lot of young adults who think of the Vietnam War as ancient history. For them, if it didn't happen within the past few years it can't have to do with the "last days." Charts that start 200 years ago are meaningless to them. Our age is one of microwaves and fast food and having everything now. Who cares about ancient history? Anything 200 years ago elicits a big "Ho-hum."

When we go to the Bible, however, we find that the last days don't just extend back 200 years. They go back 2,000 years! The New Testament consistently speaks of the first century, the time of the writing of the New Testament, as the last days. Don't take my word for it. Let's look at some texts.

The very first words of the book of Hebrews speak of the first century as the last days.

"In the past God spoke to our ancestors through the prophets at many times and in various ways, but *in these last days* he has spoken to us by his Son, whom he appointed heir of all things, and through whom also he made the universe. The Son is the radiance of God's glory and the exact representation of his being, sustaining all things by his powerful word. After he had provided purification for sins, he sat down at the right hand of the Majesty in heaven" (Hebrews 1:1-3).

Notice that the book of Hebrews contrasts the past, when God spoke in bits and pieces, with the present time of writing (the first century), when God had spoken decisively through His Son, Jesus Christ. It exalts Jesus as the one through whom God created the universe, who keeps everything functioning, and who most clearly reveals God to the world. Jesus also made a way to cleanse us from our sins (by dying on the cross), and now, by virtue of His resurrection from the dead, sits at the right hand of God in heaven. All this happened in what the biblical author calls "these last days." It was already the last days more than 1,900 years ago.

Hebrews isn't the only passage that defines the first century as the last days, however. In Acts 2, when the Holy Spirit is poured out on the apostles, people who had come from various nations heard them in their own languages, and some thought that Jesus' followers were drunk. But Peter tells them what they are seeing is not drunkenness, but from the Holy Spirit. He interprets it as a fulfillment of a prophecy in Joel that said in the "last days" God would pour out His Spirit on all people (see Joel 2:28-32).

"Then Peter stood up with the Eleven, raised his voice and addressed the crowd: 'Fellow Jews and all of you who live in Jerusalem, let me explain this to you;

listen carefully to what I say. These people are not drunk, as you suppose. It's only nine in the morning! No, this is what was spoken by the prophet Joel: . . . I will pour out my Spirit on all people" (Acts 2:14-17).

The apostle claims that what they had witnessed was evidence that it was now, in his time, the last days.

We see the same claim in the book of James. James is chiding rich Christians who are greedy and are hoarding wealth. He points out the irony of doing this in the last days, no less.

"Your wealth has rotted, and moths have eaten your clothes. Your gold and silver are corroded. Their corrosion will testify against you and eat your flesh like fire. You have hoarded wealth in the last days" (James 5:2, 3).

How can the last days last so long? Can 2,000 years ago already be the last days? If so, doesn't that make the word "last" a bit of mockery? We need to go to another passage to see why the last days began so long ago. In 1 Corinthians 15 Paul addresses some who seem to deny that there will be a future resurrection of the dead. He argues that the teaching of the resurrection of the dead is crucial and vital to our Christian faith. Note the following part of that chapter. It is a long passage, but read it carefully, for it holds the key to why the last days began so long ago.

"But if it is preached that Christ has been raised from the dead, how can some of you say that there is no resurrection of the dead? If there is no resurrection of the dead, then not even Christ has been raised. And if Christ has not been raised, our preaching is useless and so is your faith. More than that, we are then found to be false witnesses about God, for we have testified about God that he raised Christ from the dead. But he did not raise him if in fact the dead are not raised. For if the dead are not raised, then Christ has not been raised either. And if Christ has not been raised, your faith is futile; you are still in your sins. Then those also who have fallen asleep in Christ are lost. If only for this life we have hope in Christ, we are of all people most to be pitied.

"But Christ has indeed been raised from the dead, the firstfruits of those who have fallen asleep. For since death came through a man, the resurrection of the dead comes also through a man. For as in Adam all die, so in Christ all will be made alive. But each in turn: Christ, the firstfruits; then, when he comes, those who belong to him. Then the end will come, when he hands over the kingdom to God the Father after he has destroyed all dominion, authority and power. For he must reign until he has put all his enemies under his feet. The last enemy to be destroyed is death" (1 Corinthians 15:12-26).

The apostle states that the idea of the resurrection of the dead is absolutely necessary to our faith, and he ties the resurrection of Jesus together with the resurrection of believers at the end of earth's history when our Savior returns. He does so through the concept of the "firstfruits." Ancient Israel during its history would take the very first part of the harvest and present it as an offering to God. The practice did two things. It showed the nation's thanksgiving to God for the harvest, and it was also an expression of trust in God that the rest of the harvest would follow. Paul says that Jesus is already the firstfruits of the final resurrection of the dead. In other words, the resurrection of the dead has already begun with that of Jesus Christ.

Jesus' resurrection is not an isolated event. It is the beginning of God's victory over death, the destruction of the "last enemy." So if the resurrection has already begun, it is already the beginning of the last days, for the firstfruit assures us that the rest of the harvest—the resurrection of those who believe in Christ—is sure to follow.

I once heard a teacher and mentor of mine, Sakae Kubo, use an interesting illustration to help us grasp this idea. He used the analogy of lightning and thunder.

At present I live in southern California, and we don't see much lightning or hear much thunder. But for three years I lived in Atlanta, Georgia, and we could almost set our watches by the afternoon thundershowers. During the whole time we always had a lush, green lawn despite the fact that we never once watered it. The thunderstorms took care of that.

We would hear them approaching in the distance. First we would see a faint flash and then sometime later hear a soft roar. As the storm came closer, the flashes got brighter, the roars louder, and the time between them shorter. When the bang and flash were simultaneous, we knew it was upon us.

The point of comparison is this. We experience lightning and thunder at different times, because the speed of sound and light are not the same. They are actually one event, but depending on how far away we are, they seem like two separate things. It is similar with Jesus' resurrection and His second coming. Although they are really part of the same occurrence, God's victory over the power of death, we experience them at different times. Yet they are so integrally bound together that the resurrection of Jesus gives us absolute assurance that death is being defeated and our resurrection will come in turn.

With this news in hand, the world becomes a different place. We still face death, but we know that it is a defeated enemy that can keep us in the grave only temporarily. Paul calls this time "sleep." But he teaches that Jesus will awaken those who have "fallen asleep" or died, at the resurrection when He returns.

So what difference does an awareness that the resurrection of Jesus is already the beginning of the end make in our lives? First, it transforms the way we view last-day events. Instead of them being something that we follow on our charts to try to decipher when Jesus will get here, last-day events are those happenings through which God is working to defeat death and bring His kingdom to the entire universe. In other words, last-day events are not just quantitative, but qualitative. Nor are they just chronological, but theological. They are God's action to bring our salvation. And they have already begun with the resurrection of Jesus.

So if you are hoping that this book will present a chart that enables you to figure out when Jesus is coming, or exactly how Iraq and Afghanistan fit into the chronology of the end-times, you will be disappointed. In fact, if you are hoping to discover such things in the Bible, you are wasting your time. But what you will find is much more satisfying: the assurance that death is a defeated enemy and the assurance of salvation in Christ.

Now, I know you can find people who claim to have it all figured out. I've heard such scenarios all my life. I remember a preacher during the early 1970s who was absolutely convinced that the Vietnam War was Armageddon, and that before it ended Jesus would return. Another claimed that the events of September 11, 2001, would lead to the Second Coming within five years. When I was born, some of the members of the church my parents attended at the time would not congratulate them about my birth. I was born during World War II, and they told my parents that they thought it was a terrible thing they had done to bring a child into the world when the battle of Armageddon had already begun. Opening the Bible to Matthew 24, they quoted the verse that pronounces a woe on those who are nursing babies when the final troubles before the second advent of Jesus takes place. But those church members did not prove to be very good prophets.

Their failure, however, doesn't make us lose hope. If we take what the angels told Jesus' disciples seriously, we shouldn't expect humans to be able to predict when Jesus is coming. Yet this does not detract from the assurance that the end has already begun, for Jesus is alive, and we can therefore trust His promises.

Second, this good news that the resurrection of Jesus is already the beginning of the end transforms the way we view death. We love life, because God is the author of life. As a result, we do all that we can to enhance and preserve it. But we are not terrified of death, for even though it is an enemy, we know it is a defeated one that cannot have the last word. The last word is God's word of life and resurrection.

How to Survive Armageddon

Just yesterday I was at the bedside of a dying man. He is too young to be facing death, but cancer has taken its toll, and medical science can do nothing more. Certainly he doesn't want to die. While he has beautiful grandchildren that he would love to see grow up, he feels no bitterness. Instead, he has peace and calmness and thanks God for the blessings of the life he has lived. Most of all, he rests in the confidence that when Jesus comes again, our Savior will resurrect him, and he will see his family again. Although it is terribly sad to see him dying, it is also inspiring to observe the faith and confidence he has in Jesus Christ and His promised return. Here is the difference that knowing the good news about Christ's resurrection can bring into our lives.

But even the good news that the last days have already begun with the resurrection of Christ still leaves us struggling with a major question. Since we are an impatient generation; since we are people who want things now, not later; since we eat fast food and heat with microwaves; how are we supposed to keep up our hope when the last days have lasted so long? That seems to require more patience than most of us have. It will be the subject of our next chapter.

Chapter 4
HOW LONG, O LORD?

Already in the New Testament it seems that some people were concerned that Jesus had taken so long in fulfilling His promise to return. Revelation 6:10 presents a symbolic image of souls under the altar, representing the Christian martyrs, who cry out and ask how long it will be before God judges: "They called out in a loud voice, 'How long, Sovereign Lord, holy and true, until you judge the inhabitants of the earth and avenge our blood?'"

Matthew 25 presents several stories about the Second Coming. In the parable of the 10 maidens the bridegroom delays his arrival, and in the parable of the talents the master is away for a long duration. Matthew seems to be preparing his readers for a longer period of time than they had expected to pass before Jesus' return.

First, we must remember what we saw earlier in Acts 1:6-11. Jesus made it very clear to His disciples that it was not for them to know the times and seasons. Their responsibility was to witness to what He had done. But can we really keep up hope for so long? Isn't 2,000 years too long to wait?

Not if we remember that the issue is not time, but trust in God. Only God knows the time of Jesus' coming (Matthew 24:36). He hasn't asked us to count or decipher, but to trust and witness and carry on His work with faithfulness until He arrives. Admittedly this is especially hard for an impatient generation like us. But that is where trust in God carries us. God has given us the assurance of His promise by raising Jesus from the dead. We trust that since we have already seen the firstfruits, the rest will follow in God's time.

It is hard, however, for us to wait. As I said, we are not used to it. Recently I traveled from Spokane, Washington, to New York with my son and my 7-year-old grandson, Marcus. We had a short layover in Chicago. The flight from Spokane to Chicago was on time. In fact, we landed a bit early. When we got off the plane on concourse B, we looked at the big monitor to find the gate for our next flight. It was on concourse C, and beside the flight number the monitor had those two wonderful little words, "On time."

Marcus loved the walk from concourse B to C. We went down an escalator, under the runway, and went on a moving sidewalk that had neon artwork above us and the sound of chimes all around us. He wanted to do it again, and since we had time, we let him. When we went to our gate, we looked at the monitor again, only to discover that those wonderful words "On time" beside our flight number had been replaced by a not-so-wonderful word: "Canceled."

I went to a customer service counter to get help, but found no people there, only kiosks, which I couldn't get to work. Never fear, there was a phone beside the kiosk that gave a number to call if you needed personal assistance. I called the number and got a recorded message that it was no longer in service. Pulling out my cell phone, I phoned the airline and learned that it had already booked us on another flight, five hours later.

Needless to say, we were frustrated, since we had plans in New York that night and they were now ruined. Then we learned about another flight scheduled just two and a half hours later, and that we could stand by for that one. We didn't have much hope, since we were number 17 on the standby list, and after waiting a while we dropped to number 20. But just before they closed the gate they called our names, and we got on the plane. Although relieved to be on the plane, we were still frustrated. As we grumbled a bit, I told my son that at times like this I tried to remember the story of an old friend of mine. He was a long-time teacher at a college, about ready to retire, when I began teaching as a young rookie instructor at the same institution during the early 1970s.

Whenever I am frustrated at being delayed a few hours, I remember his story. He and his wife went as missionaries to South Africa in the 1930s. They finished their term, secured employment back in the United States, packed all their belongings, got tickets on a passenger ship, and were ready to return in just a few days. But their trip was delayed. The ship was late. They waited not five hours, or even five days. Not five weeks, or even five months. Their ship was delayed five years. You see, World War II broke out, the military requisitioned their ship, and the seas were not safe to travel. Five years went by. And I complain about two and a half hours!

In the mid-1980s I went to South Africa for a short teaching stint for one quarter. Before I left, this

How to Survive Armageddon

older teacher, who had now been retired for several years, asked if I would do him and his wife a favor. When they were in South Africa, they had had a baby boy who had died when he was only a few months old. They had left South Africa convinced that Jesus was coming very soon and that they would see their child again. My friend said that he and his wife were so sure about Christ's imminent return that they were willing to leave his grave there and look forward to seeing him soon. But 40 years had gone by, Jesus had not come, and they had never returned to South Africa. Now they often wondered if the grave was still there. Since I would be near that cemetery, they asked if I would try to find their son's grave.

So one afternoon in South Africa I set out to find the gravesite. It was in some disrepair, but I pulled the weeds from around it, found some flowers to put beside it, and snapped some photographs. When I returned, I took the pictures to them, and they were extremely grateful. Tears came to their eyes, and they expressed their undying trust in God and hope in the second coming of Jesus Christ. They had never imagined that 40 years would go by, but they did not waver in their hope.

Now they also rest in the grave, thousands of miles from their son, but awaiting the same resurrection.

Two weeks ago my father died, in the same eastern Washington town in which my fellow teacher had lived. When I went to choose the burial plot for my father, I purchased it without noticing the graves around it. Two days later my sister and I went to look at the place where our father was about to be buried.

To my surprise, I glanced down and saw the tombstone of my teacher friend and his wife, just a few feet from my father's grave. It was another reminder of Christian hope in the resurrection.

Our hope is based not on time but on trust that God is faithful and will fulfill His promise. We don't know how long, although in a later chapter we will see reasons we believe that we are now in the very last part of the last days and that Jesus is coming very soon. But more important than "How long" is the absolute confidence that we can trust God and know that His promise is sure. Jesus is risen. He is alive. And because of this we can have assurance. Even more amazing, such assurance is so strong that the Bible claims that the life we live in this world can already be called "eternal life." It is the subject of our next chapter.

CHAPTER 5
ETERNAL LIFE NOW

A bout 50 years ago a popular folk singing group of the day called the Kingston Trio performed a song called "The Merry Minuet." The music might have been merry, but the lyrics were not. They went like this:[*]

> "They're rioting in Africa. They're starving in
>   Spain. There's hurricanes in Florida, and
>   Texas needs rain.
> The whole world is festering with unhappy souls.
> The French hate the Germans, the Germans hate
>   the Poles.
> Italians hate Yugoslavs, South Africans hate the
>   Dutch. And I don't like anybody very much!
> But we can be tranquil and thankful and proud,
>   for man's been endowed with a mushroom-
>   shaped cloud.
> And we know for certain that some lovely day,
>   someone will set the spark off . . . and we will
>   all be blown away.
> They're rioting in Africa. There's strife in Iran.
> What nature doesn't do to us . . . will be done
>   by our fellow man."

Well, that was 50 years ago. Hardly relevant today—or is it? Some problems don't seem to change much. In fact, they get worse. We live in a world of trouble and pain. And worst of all, we dwell in a world of death.

Yet in this world where we face the threat of mushroom-shaped clouds, in this world where we see passenger planes hijacked to become weapons of mass destruction, in this world where we know that we will bury our loved ones unless they bury us first, the apostle John, writing in the New Testament, has the audacity to suggest that we can have eternal life now—in this world. We can understand how the promise of eternal life might find reality in the future, in another world, one free of sin and death. But John speaks of eternal life as a present reality for those who believe in Jesus Christ. Let's first look at several texts in which he makes his seemingly preposterous claim, and then we will try to make sense out of his message. Here are five texts about eternal life, all from either the Gospel or letters of John.

John 3:36

"Whoever believes in the Son has eternal life, but whoever rejects the Son will not see life, for God's wrath remains on them."

The apostle declares that whoever believes in or trusts the Son (God's Son, Jesus Christ) has eternal life. He doesn't state that they "might have" or "could have" eternal life. Nor does he claim that they "will have" eternal life sometime in the future. Rather, he says "has" eternal life now. Also he implies by contrast that they are free of God's wrath.

John 5:24-30

"Very truly I tell you, whoever hears my word and believes him who sent me has eternal life and will not be judged but has crossed over from death to life. Very truly I tell you, a time is coming and has now come when the dead will hear the voice of the Son of God and those who hear will live. For as the Father has life in himself, so he has granted the Son also to have life in himself. And he has given him authority to judge because he is the Son of Man.

"Do not be amazed at this, for a time is coming when all who are in their graves will hear his voice and come out—those who have done what is good will rise to live, and those who have done what is evil will rise to be condemned. By myself I can do nothing; I judge only as I hear, and my judgment is just, for I seek not to please myself but him who sent me."

Notice several things that John has to say here about the one who hears Jesus' words and believes them. First, they have eternal life. Again the tense is present. Jesus is talking about a present reality. Second, they have already passed from death to life—another present reality. He says the hour is coming and has now come when the dead will live. Obviously Jesus has in mind spiritual life and death here, because in verses 28-30 He contrasts this with the literal resurrection. Those who have eternal life not only have gone from death to life, but also will not be judged. All this is in the present.

This does not, however, negate the promise of a literal resurrection in the future. Notice that in verse 28 Jesus says the hour is coming—He does not claim that it has already arrived—when the dead who are in the graves will rise to live again.

Thus Jesus, as recorded by John, makes a distinction between eternal life and the future resurrection of the dead when Christ returns to our world. Eternal life includes the future resurrection and subsequent eternity with God, but there is also more. Eternal life also has a quality of life that the believer now possesses in Jesus Christ.

John 6:53, 54

"Jesus said to them, 'Very truly I tell you, unless you eat the flesh of the Son of Man and drink his blood, you have no life in you. Whoever eats my flesh and drinks my blood has eternal life, and I will raise them up at the last day.'"

Here we see the same idea. The believer receives spiritual nourishment through Christ and has eternal life now, and Jesus will raise them in the resurrection in the last day. Eternal life is a quality of life that we can experience at the present moment, but it also includes a future resurrection when the dead will be raised from their sleep in the grave.

John 17:3

"Now this is eternal life: that they know you, the only true God, and Jesus Christ, whom you have sent."

Here in His prayer to the Father the night before His death Jesus defines what eternal life really is. It is knowing God and His Son Jesus Christ. God, after all, is the very source of life, and when we are in connection with Him we have life—eternal life. This is the quality of life that comes from knowing God and the promise of resurrection, as well as living forever with God in the future. We look at one more text.

1 John 5:13, 14

"I write these things to you who believe in the

name of the Son of God so that you may know that you have eternal life. This is the confidence we have in approaching God: that if we ask anything according to his will, he hears us."

If we are connected to Christ, we not only have eternal life, but will know that we have it. We have confidence, because, as the old hymn by Fanny Crosby says: "Blessed assurance, Jesus is mine! O, what a foretaste of glory divine!"

When we take all these texts together, a clear message emerges. To trust in Jesus Christ as God's Son and our Savior means freedom not only from divine wrath but also from worry about the judgment. It also indicates that we have already passed from death to life, and even though we may die in this world, it is only a temporary sleep until the resurrection of the dead at the second coming of Christ when He will raise us to live with God forever.

So what difference does this make? We still live in a world of death in which we still bury our loved ones. Is this more than mere words?

I believe this message transforms life in the present in several ways. First, it frees us from preoccupation and worry about the status of our salvation and relationship with God. We have eternal life now. But it is not an arrogance that causes us to think we have it made no matter what we do. Because Christ is our source of life and hope, we must always keep our eyes focused on Him. When we pat ourselves on the back and look to our own supposed achievements, we take our gaze off Christ. Or when we kick ourselves and worry that no one who is so bad could ever be saved, we are no longer focused on our Savior. Either way, we are being self-centered and are in danger. But when we make Christ the center, we can have confidence. No longer will we have to worry about our salvation. Scripture promises that the God who began a good work in us will carry it on to completion in the day of Christ Jesus (Philippians 1:6).

Second, it changes our approach to the end-time. Instead of nervously trying to figure out which events are harbingers of the end of time, we look forward to and long for the second coming of Jesus Christ, because it means seeing Him face-to-face. We do not panic about the close of time, because we realize that we are already living the end by knowing Jesus and being in a relationship with Him now. While we do not yet have face-to-face fellowship with Jesus, our present experience with Him gives us the assurance that the face-to-face fellowship will come soon.

Finally, our assurance frees us to give our lives to God in service for His kingdom. In Matthew 10:39 Jesus says that those who find their life will lose it, but those who lose their life for Christ's sake will find it. We find true life in spending our lives for God. Our confidence in Christ frees us to take risks for the sake of God's kingdom.

It is not a matter of foolhardiness. I have a 5½-year-old grandson for whom "dangerous" is always an inviting word. If it is dangerous he wants to do it, and sometimes his desire gets in the way of his good sense. His 2½-year-old brother, on the other hand, has a very cautious side and often admonishes his older brother to be careful. My daughter sometimes refers to the younger boy as her assistant parent.

How to Survive Armageddon

God isn't asking us to take risks for the fun of it, but He invites us to give ourselves in service for others rather than selfishness. Our confidence of eternal life frees us to do so.

I think of a friend of mine who is no longer living. He grew up in and loved New York. A successful teacher and engineer in New York, he had a wonderful family with a wife and two small children. Then an invitation to leave his beloved city and his successful life and move to a little town in southeastern Washington called Walla Walla to begin an engineering program at a small Christian college disrupted his whole life. It was 1947.

Feeling that God was in the invitation, he and his family traveled across the country. The culture shock was amazing. Walla Walla, Washington, was not at all like New York (it still isn't). There he and his wife spent their first few weeks on hands and knees scrubbing an old army barracks that would serve as the venue for his new venture. But Ed Cross stayed in Walla Walla until he died and built a fully accredited, excellent engineering school that is now named after him: the Edward F. Cross School of Engineering of Walla Walla University. A plaque on the wall quotes him at his retirement: "This was not a job; it was a call from the Lord."

Our assurance of eternal life in Christ, both now and in the future, frees us to accept God's summons to give ourselves in self-sacrificial service for others and for Him.

---

* See www.sing365.com/music/lyric.nsf/The-Merry-Minuet-Lyrics-Kingston-Trio/ACA0598DAB3DOB248256BF000238FD2.

CHAPTER 6
THE VERY ELECT?

In Jesus' day messiahs were a dime a dozen. Lots of people claimed to be a messiah. We even hear of some of them in the New Testament. In Acts 5, when the Sadducees had Peter and John arrested and brought before the Jewish Council, or Sanhedrin, a wise rabbi offered some advice to the group that sought to kill the apostles.

"When they heard this, they were furious and wanted to put them to death. But a Pharisee named Gamaliel, a teacher of the law, who was honored by all the people, stood up in the Sanhedrin and ordered that the men be put outside for a little while. Then he addressed the Sanhedrin: 'Men of Israel, consider carefully what you intend to do to these men. Some time ago Theudas appeared, claiming to be somebody, and about four hundred men rallied to him. He was killed, all his followers were dispersed, and it all came to nothing. After him, Judas the Galilean appeared in the days of the census and led a band of people in revolt. He too was killed, and all his followers were scattered. Therefore, in the present case I advise you: Leave these men alone! Let them go! For if their purpose or activity is of human origin, it will fail. But if it is from God, you will not be able to stop these men; you will only find yourselves fighting against God'" (Acts 5:33-39).

How to Survive Armageddon

The two individuals he cited were hardly the only would-be messiahs. A string of them all seemed to follow the same pattern. A charismatic leader gathered a group together by making wonderful promises about how he was going to triumph over the Romans. He would brainwash the people to do whatever he said, then he would lead them to ruin. One gathered a group out by the Jordan River, and the false messiah said that it would part before them as it had for the Israelites when they first entered the land of Canaan, but it didn't, and the authorities killed them. Another assembled a group on the Mount of Olives, which overlooked the Temple, and announced that the walls of the Temple would fall as had those of Jericho after the exodus from Egypt. His promise failed, and the authorities slaughtered his followers.

When Jesus, the true Messiah, came, He knew that false messiahs would continue to lead people astray. He also recognized that before His second coming the problem of false messiahs would intensify again. So He warned His disciples.

One day on the Mount of Olives Jesus told them that the day would come when not one stone would be left on another in the Temple. The disciples were aghast. How could that be? For such a thing to happen would surely mean the end of the world. So they questioned Him.

"As Jesus was sitting on the Mount of Olives, the disciples came to him privately. 'Tell us,' they said, 'when will this happen, and what will be the sign of your coming and of the end of the age?'" (Matthew 24:3).

To them it was just one question, for they equated the destruction of the Temple with the end of the world. So when Jesus answers them throughout the rest of the chapter, some of what He says applies to the destruction of the Temple, some to the end of the world, and some to both. But even then Jesus doesn't really answer their question. They wanted to know what signs would show them when the end will come. In other words, they are worried about the *what* and the *when* questions.

Jesus redirects the issue when He replies to them. He doesn't tell them when, and He actually gives few identifiable events related to the end of the world. His concern is to warn them about false messiahs or false christs who will try to deceive them. In fact, He is so concerned about this subject that He repeats it three times in the chapter.

He begins by warning, "Watch out that no one deceives you. For many will come in my name, claiming, 'I am the Messiah,' and will deceive many" (verses 4, 5).

Jesus seeks to protect His followers, both His first-century disciples and those of the twenty-first century, from deception. In the middle of His sermon He declares, "At that time many will turn away from the faith and will betray and hate each other, and many false prophets will appear and deceive many people. Because of the increase of wickedness, the love of most will grow cold, but the one who stands firm to the end will be saved" (verses 10-13).

But even those two firm warnings were not enough. Toward the end of the sermon Jesus went into even more detail.

How to Survive Armageddon

"At that time if anyone says to you, 'Look, here is the Messiah!' or, 'There he is!' do not believe it. For false messiahs and false prophets will appear and perform great signs and wonders to deceive, if possible, even the elect. See, I have told you ahead of time.

"So if anyone tells you, 'There he is, out in the wilderness,' do not go out; or, 'Here he is, in the inner rooms,' do not believe it. For as lightning that comes from the east is visible even in the west, so will be the coming of the Son of Man" (verses 23-27).

Christ claims such counterfeits will be so clever and deceptive that they might lead astray even those who believe and trust Him. Probably most of us wouldn't claim to be the very elect, so where does that leave us? How do we keep from being deceived? Apparently Satan will do everything possible to fool or mislead us.

Fortunately, both in this chapter and in other parts of the New Testament, Jesus gives us some guidelines to protect us. If the deceptions are so clever as to deceive even the elect, we should pay careful heed to His warnings. So how do we stay safe?

Jesus gives us some basic facts that will immediately rule out most false claims to be Christ. First of all, He explains that His second coming will be visible for all to see. It will be like lightning flashing from the east to the west. Such a phenomena is hardly secret. This means that if anyone claims that Jesus has returned and there is someplace where we ought to go meet Him, it is a false Christ. Everyone will know it when He comes. He will not show up in some secret hideaway or even in an arena. His arrival will be visible for all to see.

Second, in 1 Thessalonians 4:16, 17, the Bible gives us another fact about Jesus' return that should keep us secure. It states that at His return Jesus will remain in the air while we will be brought up to Him.

"For the Lord himself will come down from heaven, with a loud command, with the voice of the archangel and with the trumpet call of God, and the dead in Christ will rise first. After that, we who are still alive and are left will be caught up together with them in the clouds to meet the Lord in the air. And so we will be with the Lord forever."

As a result, we can be assured that anyone who stands here on the earth with us and claims to be the Messiah or the returned Christ is wrong. So in giving us instruction about the manner of His return Jesus is sheltering us from deception.

The second advent of Jesus will be visible to all. Everyone will see Him. And He will gather people from the earth to join Him in the air. Such biblical facts will rule out every claim to be Christ by anyone among us on earth. It also rejects any claim by those who teach that Christ is in some secret place.

Unfortunately, when false christs emerge today the result is usually the same as back in the first century. Whether it is Jim Jones or David Koresh, people still get led to their doom. That's why such claims are so dangerous. So our first protection from deception is to know the biblical facts about the second coming of Christ.

A second safeguard is making sure that we never give over control of our thinking to someone else. Such deceivers often seek to brainwash us. But God expects us to use the mind that He endowed us with. Some people mistakenly try to set faith and Scripture on one hand over against reason and the mind on the other. But that is a false dichotomy. It is only through our minds that we come to know God, listen to Scripture, and have faith. So when Jesus walked with the two disciples on the road to Emmaus, He "opened their minds so they could understand the Scriptures" (Luke 24:45). And when Paul was concerned about the Corinthians becoming too dependent on outward signs of the Spirit, such as speaking in tongues, and making those signs rather than faith in Christ the evidence for their spiritual health, he said, "I will pray with my spirit, but I will also pray with my understanding; I will sing with my spirit, but I will also sing with my understanding" (1 Corinthians 14:15).

We serve God with our mind, and that means we never should let anyone else take over our reasoning. The first step down the road to deception is to allow someone else to do our thinking for us. The initial result is a loss of spiritual well-being, then physical disaster can occur as well. So often would-be messiahs use their mind control to lure people into adultery and other violations of divine law, and then end up causing their deaths.

God has given all of us the privilege and responsibility of thinking for ourselves, under the guidance of His Word and His Spirit. Such freedom is not always easy, and therefore it can be tempting to hand over the responsibility of living freely under God to someone else. It reminds me of a time when I did some volunteer ministry in a state penitentiary. Several inmates had recently escaped from the prison. In every case they were immediately captured. One day I asked the chaplain why so many could break out when it seemed as if the walls were quite escape-proof. He told me that the men were not escaping *from* prison but *to* prison. Sounds incredible, but he assured me it was true. He explained that in each case the inmates had been on a work detail as part of their transition to the outside world during their last few weeks of imprisonment. When he asked them why they escaped when they were going to be set free in just a couple weeks, they said they just couldn't stand it one more day. But that was not true. The chaplain said the real reason for the attempt was that they knew that when they would get caught, it would increase their sentence, and thus they would avoid having to face the responsibility of freedom. So they really escaped back into prison! Whenever we try to avoid the freedom and responsibility of using the minds God has given us, we open ourselves up for deception.

We also have yet a third safeguard. If we stay so close to Jesus that we are accustomed to His voice and can recognize it, we make it far more difficult for deception to ensnare us. By remaining connected through Bible study and prayer, we can get to know Him so well that a counterfeit would stand out like a sore thumb. Knowing Jesus and keeping close to Him is the third and most important defense.

When my now-grown daughter was just 1 year old, we found a little yellow kitten in the middle of a busy parking lot. Afraid that cars wouldn't see the kitten and that it would get hit, we rescued it. We took it home and came back the next day to knock on doors and find out to whom the kitten belonged. Sure enough, we found the home. They were sorry the kitten had gotten away, but were also trying to give it and the rest of the litter away and asked if we would like to keep the animal. Since my daughter had already fallen in love with it, we didn't have much choice.

For the next 21½ years Laura and that cat were constant companions. In the beginning she couldn't say "Kitty-cat." The closest she could come was "Dit-dat." And that became its name. It would curl up at Laura's neck and sleep. We have pictures of the same scene when she was 1, when she was 7, when she was a teenager, and when she was 21.

When Laura moved from our home to the college dormitory, the cat stayed with my wife and me, but whenever our daughter came home, the cat was right there at the door to greet her. Finally she became aged and began to fade. She lost her sense of smell, hearing, and sight, and came to the place where she could hardly get around. We had to put her food right up to her nose or she couldn't find it.

But the cat was amazing. Even though she couldn't smell, see, hear, or get around, whenever Laura returned home she was there to greet her by the time my daughter got in the door. It seemed as though something beyond her senses drew her to Laura. That's how well she knew her and how close they were.

When we stay that close to Jesus, we will not be taken in by the intense deceptions of the last days when Satan will work with such clever guile that he might also fool the very elect. Satan will even try himself to appear as an angel of light (2 Corinthians

11:14). But we can stay safe by knowing the biblical teachings about the manner of the Second Coming, by using the minds that God has given us and not letting anyone else control them by doing our thinking for us, and by staying so close to Jesus that we recognize His voice.

CHAPTER 7
NOTHING SECRET

A few days ago I drove from the church where I serve as pastor to a nearby hospital for a visit. While I waited at a stoplight I noticed that the truck in front of me had a bumper sticker. It read, "In case of rapture this truck is yours."

It's hard to know if the owner meant it in a jocular way or if the person was giving witness to a serious belief in the secret rapture, but there can be no question that many in the Christian world today take the idea quite seriously, and it is very popular. One series of 16 novels about the time of the end has sold more than 63 million copies and has been made into four movies. They all present the view that there will be a secret rapture of true believers before the second coming of Jesus.

In this chapter we will try to do four things. First, we will outline the basic idea of the rapture; second, we will look at some texts used to support the belief; third, we will examine them within their context to see what they truly teach; and finally we will ask the question "So what?"

What is this belief in the secret rapture all about? Here is the basic scenario. Those who hold it teach that seven years before the actual second coming of Christ God will simply snatch the true followers of Jesus Christ from the earth and take them home with

Him. Life will continue on the earth, but the true believers will suddenly disappear. It enables them to skip the terrible time of tribulation that will take place during the seven years until Jesus arrives in the clouds.

According to this view, during the seven years the antichrist will rule, leading to persecution, calamity, and trouble such as has never been seen before. But the true believers will be spared. Also during this time the Temple in Jerusalem will be rebuilt, and according to some, all Jews will be converted to Christ. Also during this time Christians who had not been prepared for the rapture will have a second chance. If they endure through the tribulation and are faithful to God, they can then be saved at the visible Second Coming.

Supporters of the rapture point to several biblical texts as evidence for their position. One is Matthew 24:40, 41: "Two men will be in the field; one will be taken and the other left. Two women will be grinding with a hand mill; one will be taken and the other left."

They interpret the verse to mean that two people will be side by side and all of a sudden one of them will simply be gone. To them the text is speaking about the sudden disappearance of all those who are true believers at the time of the rapture.

Another passage used for support of the teaching is 1 Corinthians 15:51, 52 in which Paul declares that believers will be changed in an instant. "Listen, I tell you a mystery: We will not all sleep, but we will all be changed—in a flash, in the twinkling of an eye."

Secret rapture advocates regard the verse as referring to the instantaneous rapture that will occur at the beginning of the tribulation. People will simply be going about their normal business in life when all of a sudden they will vanish. Furthermore, many see the words "caught up" in 1 Thessalonians 4:17 as a reference of God's sudden taking of true Christians to heaven: "After that, we who are still alive and are left will be caught up together with them in the clouds to meet the Lord in the air."

When we look at all three verses in context, however, we discover quite a different picture. We find that there is nothing secret about the events described. In fact, all of them point to the same event, which is the second coming of Christ, a happening that will be visible to all. Let's look at the evidence.

First, notice Jesus' words in Matthew 24:26–31. His disciples have asked Him about the destruction of Jerusalem and the end of the world. As we have seen previously, some of His comments refer to one aspect, some to the other, and some to both. But none of them speak of a secret rapture before the Second Coming. Read the following passage carefully:

"So if anyone tells you, 'There he is, out in the wilderness,' do not go out; or, 'Here he is, in the inner rooms,' do not believe it. For as lightning that comes from the east is visible even in the west, so will be the coming of the Son of Man. Wherever there is a carcass, there the vultures will gather.

"Immediately after the distress of those days

  'the sun will be darkened,

  and the moon will not give its light;

  the stars will fall from the sky,

  and the heavenly bodies will be shaken.'

"Then will appear the sign of the Son of Man in

heaven. And then all the peoples of the earth will mourn when they see the Son of Man coming on the clouds of heaven, with power and great glory. And he will send his angels with a loud trumpet call, and they will gather his elect from the four winds, from one end of the heavens to the other."

Let's consider several elements associated with the series of events that Jesus describes in Matthew:

It is visible, just like lightning flashing from the east to the west.

The peoples of the earth mourn.

The Son of Man (Jesus Christ) comes.

He comes with power and glory.

There is a trumpet call.

The people are gathered to meet Christ.

Clearly nothing is secret here. The Second Coming is visible, audible, and manifests itself with great power and glory. This fits with what we find in Revelation 1:7 as well:

> "'Look, he is coming with the clouds,
>   and every eye will see him,
>   even those who pierced him';
>   and all peoples on earth 'will mourn
>   because of him.' So shall it be! Amen."

John's prophecy here of the Second Advent is obviously the same event as Matthew 24, because it also includes the peoples of the earth mourning and the visible nature of Christ's arrival (every eye will see Him). Since Matthew 24:40, 41 parallels this, we should see it as commentary on what happens at the second coming of Christ, not something seven years before it. When Jesus declares that one is taken and the other left, He is simply pointing out the fact that not all will be saved when He returns. He is not implying that it will be an instantaneous disappearance before the Second Advent.

So we begin to see a collection of events associated with the return of Jesus Christ. They include the trumpet call and the open, visible nature of His arrival. It is significant therefore that when we look at the two passages from Paul (1 Corinthians 15 and 1 Thessalonians 4), we also find the trumpet call, showing that they speak of the same event. We find it further confirmed by the fact that the resurrection of the dead also appears in both passages, and the final resurrection of the dead occurs at the second coming of Christ (see chapter 3).

When we look at 1 Corinthians 15, we have to read on from verse 51. Notice what we find in verse 52:

"Listen, I tell you a mystery: We will not all sleep, but we will all be changed—in a flash, in the twinkling of an eye, *at the last trumpet. For the trumpet will sound,* the dead will be raised imperishable, and we will be changed."

Scripture does not associate the instantaneous change with a secret rapture seven years before the Second Coming. It takes place at the Second Advent, when the trumpet sounds and the dead are raised—the same event described in Matthew 24.

Now notice how well all this fits with 1 Thessalonians 4:15-18.

"According to the Lord's word, we tell you that we who are still alive, who are left until the coming of the Lord, will certainly not precede those who have fallen asleep. For the Lord himself will come down from heaven, with a loud command, with the voice of the archangel *and with the trumpet call of God,* and the dead in Christ will rise first. After that, we who are still alive and are left will be caught up together with them in the clouds to meet the Lord in the air. And so we will be with the Lord forever. Therefore encourage one another with these words."

The passage presents a clear sequence. Paul says that those who are alive will not go to heaven ahead of those who have died. But if believers are raptured seven years before the Second Coming and the resurrection that occurs then, those still alive *would* ascend to heaven before those who died—in fact, seven years earlier. The apostle goes on to add that the Lord will come down from heaven with a loud command and divine trumpet call, elements that tie this event with the series of happenings that we have already seen associated with the Second Coming. Especially crucial is Paul's clear teaching that the saints being "caught up" in the clouds occurs *after* the visible return of Jesus and the resurrection of the dead. Therefore being "caught up" cannot possibly refer to a secret rapture that takes place seven years before the Second Advent. It is inextricably tied to the other events associated with the second coming of Christ.

So what happens when Christ returns? He comes in a way that is visible to all. Every eye sees Him. In addition to the visible display, an audible trumpet awakens the dead in Christ while He remains above the earth. First, the righteous dead are resurrected and caught up to meet Him. Then those who are still living at the time of His return join them. Finally Christ takes both groups to be with Him forever.

At least some of the basic elements of this unified picture appear in each of the biblical passages sometimes used to support the idea of the secret rapture. But all the passages fit together into a coherent whole. They all refer to one event, the second coming of Jesus Christ. There is nothing secret here.

What about the seven-year period of tribulation, however? Those who hold belief in a secret rapture take the duration from the prophecy in Daniel 9:25-27. It reads:

"Know therefore and understand, that from the going forth of the commandment to restore and to build Jerusalem unto the Messiah the Prince shall be seven weeks, and threescore and two weeks: the street shall be built again, and the wall, even in troublous times.

"And after threescore and two weeks shall Messiah be cut off, but not for himself: and the people of the prince that shall come shall destroy the city and the sanctuary; and the end thereof shall be with a flood, and unto the end of the war desolations are determined.

"And he shall confirm the covenant with many for one week: and in the midst of the week he shall cause the sacrifice and the oblation to cease, and for the overspreading of abominations he shall make it desolate, even until the consummation, and that determined shall be poured upon the desolate" (KJV).

The passage refers to a time period of seven weeks, 62 weeks, and one week, which totals 70 weeks, or 490 days. Those who teach the secret rapture interpret these days as prophetic days that represent a year, and they do have good biblical precedent for it. The prophecy would begin at the time of the command to restore and rebuild Jerusalem, an event that occurred in 457 B.C. The 69 weeks of years, multiplied by seven, would represent 483 years and would take us to A.D. 27. What does the prophecy say happens then? It is the time of the Messiah or anointed one, which in the language of the New Testament is "Christ." That seems to fit. So far it is quite clear and those who hold to the rapture are correct in their interpretation of the passage. The difficulty comes in their understanding of the seventieth week.

Those who advocate a secret rapture cut the seventieth week off from the other 69 and introduce a 2,000-year gap from A.D. 27 until the rapture. But nothing in the text suggests such an interval. Rather, it speaks of the week when the Messiah or Christ confirms the covenant He had made with His people to be their God. Therefore the seventieth week has to do with Christ's ministry on earth, not some event 2,000 years later. The fact that the sacrifice ceases in the middle of the week refers to His death, which brought an end to the need for further sacrifice. Daniel does not support the idea of a seven-year tribulation after a gap of many centuries. The entire 70 weeks are contiguous, and the seventieth week involves the period of Jesus' ministry on earth, His death in the middle of the week, and the gospel going to the Gentiles at the end of that week.

Another element of the rapture teaching is the belief in the rebuilding of the Temple in Jerusalem before Christ returns, which those who support the rapture see occurring during the seven years of tribulation. One of the prophecies used to support it is Zechariah 1:14-17. It certainly does call for the Temple in Jerusalem to be rebuilt.

"Then the angel who was speaking to me said, 'Proclaim this word: This is what the Lord Almighty says: "I am very jealous for Jerusalem and Zion, but I am very angry with the nations that feel secure. I was only a little angry, but they went too far with the punishment."

"'Therefore this is what the Lord says: "I will return to Jerusalem with mercy, and there my house will be rebuilt. And the measuring line will be stretched out over Jerusalem," declares the Lord Almighty.

"'Proclaim further: This is what the Lord Almighty says: "My towns will again overflow with prosperity, and the Lord will again comfort Zion and choose Jerusalem."'"

The questions raised are: what rebuilding is the passage talking about, and when does (or did) it occur? If we read just a few verses earlier in Zechariah 1:7 we see that the prophecy is dated: "On the twenty-fourth day of the eleventh month, the month of Shebat, in the second year of Darius, the word of the Lord came to the prophet Zechariah son of Berekiah, the son of Iddo."

Rendered in modern dating, it turns out to be February of 519 B.C. When Zechariah received the prophecy in 519, the Temple in Jerusalem was in ruins. The Babylonians had destroyed Jerusalem and its Temple in 586 B.C. and taken the Jews into captivity. So during the time of Zechariah the Temple did need rebuilding. Therefore it is logical to assume that the prophecy concerns the reconstruction of the

Jerusalem Temple of his day. And the prophecy was fulfilled. It took a while, but we read about the rebuilding in the biblical books of Ezra and Nehemiah. Thus the prophecy was not about the end-time, but about Zechariah's era.

Nothing in Scripture ties the rebuilding of the Temple to the end-time. In fact, there is great danger in wresting Old Testament prophecies from their original context and plopping them down in the last days.

God had a plan for Israel, one that He revealed through the prophets. Not all of the prophecies relating to it were fulfilled, however, because some of them depended on the people's response. For instance, Zechariah goes on to prophesy that it was God's desire that once Israel had rebuilt the Temple, all the nations would flock to Jerusalem and want to follow Israel's God (see, for example, Zechariah 8:23: "This is what the Lord Almighty says: 'In those days ten people from all languages and nations will take firm hold of one Jew by the hem of his robe and say, "Let us go with you, because we have heard that God is with you"'").

Unfortunately, God's people did not always reach out to the world as He intended. They became exclusive. Those aspects of prophecy that depend on human action are conditional, because God doesn't force humans. We see a clear example of the conditional nature of His prophecies in the book of Jonah. Jonah prophesied that Nineveh would be destroyed in 40 days. But the people repented, so the prophecy did not come to pass—something that Jonah had been worried about all along. That was at least part of the reason for his reluctance to go to Nineveh in the first place. So also not all of the prophecies about Israel were fulfilled in the precise way that God had predicted, because they were at least in part dependent on how the people responded to them. In principle many of these prophecies did meet their fulfillment in Christ, but that does not mean that they also involve the end-time.

Indeed, it does a disservice to apply prophecies intended for the Jews in Old Testament times to the end of time. They were not addressing the modern state of Israel, but God's people then. Many times New Testament writers will use the language from such prophecies to show how God will ultimately fulfill their intent. For example, in Isaiah 65:17-21 the prophet speaks of a new heaven and a new earth.

> "See, I will create
>> new heavens and a new earth.
>> The former things will not be remembered,
>> nor will they come to mind.
>> But be glad and rejoice forever
>> in what I will create,
>> for I will create Jerusalem to be a delight
>> and its people a joy.
>> I will rejoice over Jerusalem
>> and take delight in my people;
>> the sound of weeping and of crying
>> will be heard in it no more.
> "Never again will there be in it
>> an infant who lives but a few days,
>> or an old man who does not live out his years;
>> the one who dies at a hundred
>> will be thought a mere child;

the one who fails to reach a hundred
    will be considered accursed.
They will build houses and dwell in them;
    they will plant vineyards and eat their fruit."

Although this looks like a prophecy of the new heavens and new earth when Jesus comes the second time, certain elements in it don't fit. For instance, in the new earth death will not exist at all, whereas here the promise is that people will live a long time before they die. This prophecy was intended for Israel, but because of the unfaithfulness of the people it was never fulfilled exactly as predicted. But God doesn't give up. He does something even better—He promises a new heaven and new earth with no death at all. So John, in Revelation 21 and 22, takes the language of this prophecy and makes it even better. But it would be a mistake to try to assign all the literal details of the Isaiah prophecy to the end-time and the new earth that God is preparing for us.

One of the problems of the secret rapture theory is that its adherents take many Old Testament prophecies and apply them to the last days and the modern state of Israel in ways inconsistent with their original context. When we take the original setting into view, no prophecy predicts the rebuilding of the Temple in Jerusalem before the second coming of Christ.

Even if the secret rapture theory is not biblical, what difference does it make whether you believe Jesus will arrive seven years after a rapture or whether you believe there will be no rapture first?

The secret rapture theory has several dangers inherent in it. One is the false expectation of a second chance for making a decision to follow Christ fully after the rapture. If you don't make the rapture, you've still got another opportunity to be saved. It gives a false security that can lull us into thinking that what we do *now* is not all that important. Of course, our motivation for following Christ should always be our love for Him and our appreciation for His free gift of grace, not fear of the future. Nevertheless, it is important to know that the present counts.

Another threat is the problem of being distracted from the true issues in the plan of salvation and focusing instead on political scenarios, government conspiracies, and speculative ideas, rather than trust in Christ. For example, I heard a radio preacher recently say that if you want to be prepared for the rapture and the Second Coming, keep your eyes fixed on the Middle East. Wouldn't it be a whole lot better to remain focused on Christ and His Word?

Many who believe in the rapture also spend a lot of time speculating about who the antichrist will be and what he will do. Yet the picture of a single antichrist at the end of time is not in keeping with what the Bible teaches, as we will see in the following chapter.

You may be tempted to say, "With all these views and conflicting interpretations, how can we ever be prepared to meet Christ at His coming?" Our only safety is to keep our gaze centered on Christ and the messages that He has given us in His Word. God loves us and doesn't want anyone to be lost. He will guide us if we ask Him. When we pray for the Spirit He will show us the truth of His Word and keep us secure.

Remember that He is on our side and our only safety.

About a year ago my wife went from our home in southern California to Seattle to visit our daughter and her family. She flew into Sea-Tac Airport south of Seattle, rented a car, and then drove to Lynnwood, north of Seattle, where our daughter lives. It was late at night.

I was already in bed asleep when a phone call from my wife awakened me. "Help me; I'm lost!" she announced. Not liking the idea of my wife wandering around alone late at night, I asked her to describe where she was. What were the landmarks that would help me identify her location? "You know that big U-Haul truck lot? I saw that," she said.

I told her that was great. It was only a mile from her destination. Where was she in relationship to it? Well, she said she had seen it 20 minutes before but couldn't figure out how to get off the freeway, somehow got turned around, and now had no idea where she was. I told her to look for a freeway sign so I would at least know which freeway she was on. Finally she spotted one telling her that she was on the 405.

I blurted out, "The 405! You don't go on the 405 to get to their house. If you were already within a mile of their house, how did you get where you are? You are a good 10 miles away! How could you do that?" For some reason she didn't appreciate that line of questioning and said, "Just get me to their house." So I turned on the computer, figured out right where she was, and directed her to the gate of our daughter's condo. With the map program and the phone I got her right there.

And I was happy to do it. I love my wife and didn't want her lost out there late at night. God loves us even more and doesn't want us to grope in darkness. That's why He has given us His Word, His Spirit, and His promise to be with us. If we keep our eyes focused on Him, He will guide us safely to His kingdom.

What about the danger of the antichrist, however? It might be comforting and helpful to see what the Bible actually says about this figure. That is the subject of our next chapter.

Chapter 8
THE ANTICHRIST

For several years I taught a college class on the book of Revelation. Although I enjoyed the class, it was something of a hazard. Since I was the teacher, everyone assumed I was an expert on Revelation and showered me with questions, many of which I must confess that I couldn't answer. One subject that people often asked about was the antichrist. Who will the antichrist be? When will he come? How will we know him? What will he do? Since I taught about the book, certainly I should know about the antichrist.

Most of the questioners were quite surprised, however, when I told them that the word "antichrist" never appears in the book of Revelation. It is true, as we shall see later, that the concept may appear, but the word itself doesn't—not anywhere in the book of Revelation. There are beasts and various powers that Satan uses, and without doubt these powers oppose Christ, but the book calls none of them explicitly "antichrist."

That is not the only surprise that the New Testament offers about the antichrist, however. Some are even more startled to find that the New Testament speaks of the antichrist not in terms of future, but of past and present. We usually think of the antichrist as a figure that will appear just before the return of Christ, but the New Testament mentions antichrists who have already come.

And that brings us to the third surprise. We usually think about the antichrist (singular), but the New Testament talks about antichrists (plural). There is not just *an* antichrist, but *many* antichrists.

Please don't take my word for it. Let's look together at the New Testament evidence. Only two books in the New Testament explicitly mention the antichrist: the two letters of John, the ones we call 1 John and 2 John.

In order to see the New Testament material clearly, let's begin by looking at each passage and simply noticing interesting facts that we see in the passage. After we have briefly surveyed all three, we will be able to summarize the New Testament teaching about the antichrist and ask what it means for us. First we will examine 1 John 2:18-27:

"Dear children, this is the last hour; and as you have heard that the antichrist is coming, even now many antichrists have come. This is how we know it is the last hour. They went out from us, but they did not really belong to us. For if they had belonged to us, they would have remained with us; but their going showed that none of them belonged to us.

"But you have an anointing from the Holy One, and all of you know the truth. I do not write to you because you do not know the truth, but because you do know it and because no lie comes from the truth. Who is the liar? It is whoever denies that Jesus is the Christ. Such a person is the antichrist—denying the Father and the Son. No one who denies the Son has the Father; whoever acknowledges the Son has the Father also.

"As for you, see that what you have heard from the beginning remains in you. If it does, you also will remain in the Son and in the Father. And this is what he promised us—eternal life.

"I am writing these things to you about those who are trying to lead you astray. As for you, the anointing you received from him remains in you, and you do not need anyone to teach you. But as his anointing teaches you about all things and as that anointing is real, not counterfeit—just as it has taught you, remain in him."

Several interesting facts emerge about the antichrist from this passage. First, John makes it clear that his readers have already heard about the antichrist before he writes to them. He is not introducing a new concept. The apostle also regards his own era as the last hour, a time when Christians can expect to see the fulfillment of prophecies they have heard in the past. We also notice that the antichrist here is plural. John sees a whole group of people whom he designates as antichrists. Sharing several characteristics, they appear to be former Christians. Once part of John's fellowship, they have left him and now deny that Jesus is the Christ, or the Messiah. As a result the apostle sees what they have done as a repudiation of both the Father and the Son. These people not only reject such basic tenets of the Christian faith; they also lead other people astray through their false doctrine.

John returns to this subject of the antichrist in 1 John 4:1-6:

"Dear friends, do not believe every spirit, but test the spirits to see whether they are from God, because many false prophets have gone out into the world.

How to Survive Armageddon

This is how you can recognize the Spirit of God: Every spirit that acknowledges that Jesus Christ has come in the flesh is from God, but every spirit that does not acknowledge Jesus is not from God. This is the spirit of the antichrist, which you have heard is coming and even now is already in the world.

"You, dear children, are from God and have overcome them, because the one who is in you is greater than the one who is in the world. They are from the world and therefore speak from the viewpoint of the world, and the world listens to them. We are from God, and whoever knows God listens to us; but whoever is not from God does not listen to us. This is how we recognize the Spirit of truth and the spirit of falsehood."

Here John sets forth some criteria for testing doctrines and those who present them. Faithful Christians will acknowledge that Jesus Christ has come in the flesh. The apostle declares that those who oppose this Christian affirmation represent the spirit of the antichrist. Again John confirms that his readers have already heard that the antichrist is coming and again he emphasizes that it has already arrived. But along with this affirmation comes an assurance as well. God's power is greater than the spirit of the antichrist and therefore believers need not fear it.

Only one other reference to the specific word "antichrist" appears in the New Testament aside from these two passages in 1 John. It comes from 2 John, a short letter of just 14 verses. After setting forth the great love command that we also find in the Gospel of John and 1 John, the apostle then warns his readers about false teachers.

"I say this because many deceivers, who do not acknowledge Jesus Christ as coming in the flesh, have gone out into the world. Any such person is the deceiver and the antichrist. Watch out that you do not lose what we have worked for, but that you may be rewarded fully. Anyone who runs ahead and does not continue in the teaching of Christ does not have God; whoever continues in the teaching has both the Father and the Son" (2 John 7-9).

John refers here to the same problem that he addressed in 1 John. Some who were originally part of their fellowship no longer acknowledged Christ as coming in the flesh. Again he uses the word "antichrist" to refer to them, and again he makes the word plural. Many deceivers have gone out, and as far as the apostle is concerned, anyone who contributes to such deception is the antichrist.

What are we to make of the references to "antichrist" in the New Testament? Do they have any significance for us today? To answer, let's explore in more detail some of the facts that we have already noted.

First, it is intriguing that John sees his own day as the last hour, a fact that we have already encountered in chapter 3. For New Testament writers, the resurrection of Jesus Christ was already the beginning of the end. It was the firstfruits that gave absolute assurance that the end would come. Jesus' promise of His return would be fulfilled. The world was already a different place, because the final victory had been won in the crucifixion and the resurrection. Now, Christians awaited the day when that victory would fully manifest itself at Christ's second coming. Thus it was no wonder for John that with the dawn of the new era those events predicted for the last days should be already evident in the world. And that included the appearance of antichrists.

Second, we have already seen how the apostle makes it clear that people were already expecting the antichrist. He was not introducing something that they had never heard of before. We, of course, do not have any specific prediction using the word "antichrist," but certainly one important background was what Jesus Himself had said. When we look at Mark 13 and the parallel record of His speech in Matthew 24, we find that the Savior predicted that false christs and false messiahs would emerge. Undoubtedly His prediction led to the expectation that antichrists would come. We also find other New Testament writers referring to the same concept but in different words. In 2 Thessalonians 2 Paul foretells the arrival of a man of lawlessness. And, of course, the book of Revelation speaks of various beasts, entities on earth that carry out the work and will of the great dragon beast, Satan himself (see Revelation 12 and 13, for example). In other words, John is in line with a whole stream of Christian teaching in the early church. But now, under God's inspiration, John applies that teaching to his own present circumstances.

Next we notice the specific issue in question. Those whom John labels as antichrists deny that Jesus Christ has come in the flesh. In other words, they reject Jesus as the Christ. When we read John's letters it is much as if we are listening to one side of a telephone conversation. We don't really know exactly what those opponents were saying, or even exactly who they were, but we can have some idea. For example, some in the early church attempted to blend their Christian faith with certain pagan teachings of the time. They eventually became known as Gnostics. One of their basic beliefs was a dualism that saw matter as evil. Often they viewed the creation of the material world as a part of an unfortunate act by a lesser evil god, who corrupted life by imprisoning sparks of divinity within matter.

Naturally those who accepted such things could hardly believe that Jesus was truly human and divine. A divine Christ for them could not really be human and live in human flesh. Early Christian Gnostics had different ways of getting around the idea of the Incarnation, or the teaching that the Word became flesh (John 1:14). Some said that Jesus was not really human, but only *appeared* to be human. Others taught that the divine Christ adopted the body of Jesus only temporarily. But common to Gnosticism was the view that Jesus Christ could not be both truly divine and truly human.

We don't really know if the opponents in John were Gnostics, or if they simply shared some of the same viewpoints that Gnostics had. At any rate, the history of Gnosticism in the church shows how it would be possible for the apostle to encounter people who denied that Jesus was the Christ.

Finally we notice that John takes a bold step. He sees whoever the individuals were as a fulfillment of the antichrist to come. Their false teachings and especially their attempts to deceive others and lead

How to Survive Armageddon

Christians astray by turning them away from Jesus Christ participated in the spirit of the antichrist. For John the antichrist was more than just one particular figure who would surface at a given time. It obviously included the spirit of Satan's work to challenge Christ and lead people away from their Savior.

What does it all mean for us today? Currently a lot of speculation rages around the concept of a future antichrist. To many people it has become an obsession to figure out exactly who the antichrist is and where he will appear. But if we take John seriously, the whole subject of the antichrist is broader than that. The danger of the antichrist does not just threaten people at one particular time only. Instead, there is a *continual* danger that we might be deceived and participate in the spirit of the antichrist. In fact, if we take John's wording seriously, any one of us can be antichrist, if we lead people astray from a genuine belief in Jesus Christ as Savior.

In other words, it is vital what we believe and teach, not necessarily in a mere abstract and theoretical way, but in relationship to our central affirmation that Jesus Christ is our Savior. Many forces and powers in the world may attempt to lure us away from our faith in Jesus Christ. We must be continually on guard. As the book of Revelation shows us, Satan can work through individuals as well as religious institutions and political entities to erase our commitment to Christ. Each one of them, according to John, can be labeled "antichrist."

But even though we do have to be on continual guard, it is terribly important that we remember the assurance that John repeatedly gives us. Christ's power is sufficient to keep us from both evil and falsehood. If we are committed to Him, it really is true that the One in us is greater than the one who works through the antichrists.

You see, when the New Testament talks about the antichrist, the bottom line isn't merely a secret code that we must figure out so that we will know exactly when the antichrist arrives and who he will be. Rather, it is a warning to be on continuous guard against the spirit of antichrist, coupled with the assurance that if we keep our focus on Jesus Christ, we have already overcome that spirit of antichrist and need not be afraid.

When we look at all the problems in the world, the temptations to evil, and the destructive actions and teachings that Satan uses, what a blessing it is to remember that the One who is in us (Christ) is greater than the one who is in the world (Satan, who stands behind the spirit of antichrist). In Jesus Christ we have overcome.

CHAPTER 9
SIGNS OF THE KINGDOM

Years ago I was getting my hair cut in the state of Michigan, where I was going to school. The barber asked me where I lived, and I told him southern California. "I could never live there," he replied. "Why, I wouldn't even visit there!" When I asked him why, he said, "Because of all the earthquakes." Even though I told him that lots more people died every year from tornadoes in the Midwest than from earthquakes in California, he wasn't convinced.

When the disciples questioned Jesus about signs of His coming and the end of the world, He spoke about earthquakes, but what He said is surprising. We often think about such catastrophes as earthquakes, famines, and wars as signs of the end, but Jesus turns things upside down. We read about the discussion in Matthew 24:1-3.

"Jesus left the temple and was walking away when his disciples came up to him to call his attention to its buildings. 'Do you see all these things?' he asked. 'Truly I tell you, not one stone here will be left on another; every one will be thrown down.' As Jesus was sitting on the Mount of Olives, the disciples came to him privately. 'Tell us,' they said, 'when will this happen, and what will be the sign of your coming and of the end of the age?'"

As we already noticed in chapter 6, the disciples raised a complex issue. It really consisted of two questions about two different things. The two questions were "When?" and "What will be the sign of Your coming and the end of the age?" So "when" and "what are the signs" were the disciples' concern. But it involved two different aspects: the destruction of the Temple in Jerusalem and the return of Christ at the end of the age. They probably thought of both as just one event. For them, if the Temple fell, it must be the end of the world. As a result they didn't realize that the two would be centuries apart.

Jesus' answer is also an involved one. It is difficult because He blends the two events in His response. Some of what He said obviously focused on the destruction of Jerusalem, which took place in A.D. 70. For example, His instruction to flee from Judea was localized to a specific area where the destruction of the Temple occurred. But His statement that His coming would be like lightning from the east to the west for all to see was clearly not restricted to Jerusalem and had to do with His second advent.

His answer is also complex in still another way, because He doesn't directly answer their question. As we saw in chapter 6, Jesus began by warning them about false messiahs and prophets. After that, He turned to catastrophes usually considered as signs of the coming of the Messiah. But He seemed to change the focus by saying that such things were not signs. Notice Matthew 24:6-8.

"You will hear of wars and rumors of wars, but see to it that you are not alarmed. Such things must happen, but the end is still to come. Nation will rise against nation, and kingdom against kingdom. There will be famines and earthquakes in various places. All these are the beginning of birth pains."

Jesus tells us not to get excited when we see these things. The end is not yet. They are just what will happen along the way while we are waiting for Him. Such events are only the beginning. As we then proceed through the chapter Jesus doesn't really give the disciples very much in the way of signs that they can use to calculate the time of His arrival. He uses the word "sign" only two more times in the chapter. The first is in Matthew 24:24, in which He speaks of the signs and wonders that the false messiahs will do, and the second is in Matthew 24:30, 31, in which He actually refers to His return as a sign:

"Then will appear the sign of the Son of Man in heaven. And then all the peoples of the earth will mourn when they see the Son of Man coming on the clouds of heaven, with power and great glory. And he will send his angels with a loud trumpet call, and they will gather his elect from the four winds, from one end of the heavens to the other."

The true "sign" is Jesus coming again and bringing the promised kingdom with its victory over sin and death. So instead of giving a list of indicators that the disciples could use to calculate the time of Christ's return, He says the true sign will be the return itself.

The New Testament employs the word "sign" in different ways. Many times Jesus used it in a negative manner to refer to the miracles that people wanted Him to perform to prove His claims as to who He was. An example appears in Matthew 12:38-41:

"Then some of the Pharisees and teachers of the law said to him, 'Teacher, we want to see a sign from you.'

"He answered, 'A wicked and adulterous generation asks for a sign! But none will be given it except the sign of the prophet Jonah. For as Jonah was three days and three nights in the belly of a huge fish, so the Son of Man will be three days and three nights in the heart of the earth. The men of Nineveh will stand up at the judgment with this generation and condemn it; for they repented at the preaching of Jonah, and now something greater than Jonah is here.'"

The Pharisees and teachers of religious law wanted Jesus to do something spectacular, but He refused, because He knew that merely being wowed would not lead anyone to true repentance. Only recognizing that He was their Savior and that He would die for them and be resurrected could change their hearts. An impressive sign would leave them only wanting something even more dramatic tomorrow.

It is the same with the signs of the end. People initially stirred by events that supposedly show that Jesus' coming is just around the corner often lose their enthusiasm when the excitement wears off and time passes. Jesus didn't want people to follow Him because they saw spectacular miracles or because they were sure that His second coming was imminent. Rather, He desired that they accept Him because they recognized that they were sinners in need of a Savior, and that He had come from God to be that Savior. He longed for them to see the issues involved in the battle between God and Satan for the minds of human beings. Only this would lead to true repentance and a new life.

Yet even though Jesus refused to dole out signs like magic tricks for the Pharisees and religious teachers, He did perform miracles, and the Gospel of John calls such miracles "signs." John records seven miracles, and usually they are tied to Jesus' teaching about who He is and how He has come to save. For example, in John 6 Jesus feeds 5,000 people with just five loaves and two fish offered by a little boy. Afterward He speaks of Himself as the bread of life that has come into the world. In John 8 Jesus speaks about being the light of the world. Then in John 9 He opens the eyes of a blind man as a demonstration of what the light of the world does. Finally, in John 11, Jesus claims to be the resurrection and the life. Afterward He raises Lazarus from the dead.

The "signs" in John show that through Jesus' ministry the kingdom of God is breaking into our world. They point to the ultimate sign when Jesus will return and bring sin and death to an end.

What, therefore, is Jesus trying to tell His disciples in Matthew 24 when they ask about the signs leading up to the Second Coming? He doesn't really give them a list of events that will enable them to calculate how close they are to His return. In light of how He responded to Pharisees who were looking for a sign, it should hardly surprise us that Jesus changes the focus to the kind of lives He wants the disciples to live. We see this especially when we come to the end of Matthew 24. Instead of telling how to figure out the time of the end, He explains that, regardless of the time, they should be faithful to Him and live according to the principles and values He has taught them. To get this across Jesus uses two analogies, both of which have to do with faithful servants. Look at Matthew 24:42-51:

"Therefore keep watch, because you do not know on what day your Lord will come. But understand this: If the owner of the house had known at what time of night the thief was coming, he would have kept watch and would not have let his house be broken into. So you also must be ready, because the Son of Man will come at an hour when you do not expect him.

"Who then is the faithful and wise servant, whom the master has put in charge of the servants in his household to give them their food at the proper time? It will be good for that servant whose master finds him doing so when he returns. Truly I tell you, he will put him in charge of all his possessions. But suppose that servant is wicked and says to himself, 'My master is staying away a long time,' and he then begins to beat his fellow servants and to eat and drink with drunkards. The master of that servant will come on a day when he does not expect him and at an hour he is not aware of. He will cut him to pieces and assign him a place with the hypocrites, where there will be weeping and gnashing of teeth."

When someone goes away and leaves a servant in charge, they don't want the servant to be faithful only when they think the master is about to return. Servants should be faithful because they care for the master and take the responsibility given them seriously. Jesus wants His disciples to serve Him because they love Him and desire to do His will, not simply because He might show up at any moment. Our relationship with Him should be based on our appreciation for the grace that He has freely poured out to us.

In Matthew 25 Jesus goes on to tell three more stories that further illustrate the kind of way He wants the disciples to live. It involves commitment to Him, the responsible use of the gifts He gives, and care and concern for other people. In other words, He wants His followers to begin now already living according to the principles and values of God's kingdom. (We will say much more about this in chapter 13.)

We often think of our world and God's kingdom as totally separate—that God's kingdom is up there in heaven and our world is down here where we live. But in Jesus' ministry we already see an overlap between the two. In Him the kingdom already begins to break into this world. And when we live according to the values of His kingdom, we in a sense are signs of that kingdom. We give witness to what it is all about and let people know that it is coming.

Of course we realize that we could never totally bring God's kingdom to this world, for His promise is that *He* will end all sin and death. But we can present a foretaste of what the kingdom is all about and help draw others to God so that they will be prepared to enter it. When we do this, we actually become signs of the kingdom. The signs are not simply events that point to Christ's coming, but the lives of people who witness to the world as to what God's kingdom is like.

It is a realm whose values are upside down from most of this world. Humility rather than hubris, generosity rather than greed, and service rather than status all rule. Jesus calls on His disciples to live out the values of His kingdom right now and thus become impressive signs of what the kingdom is all about and of the reality of the promise that it is coming. And this faithful witness to the kingdom comes not because of a fixed chronological sequence of time, but because of a commitment to Jesus.

Does this mean that time doesn't matter at all? that we should never emphasize the nearness of Christ's coming? Even though our faithfulness to God should be a constant, not based on the time of His appearing, it would be foolish of us to ignore the abundant evidence that we are living in the very final part of the last days and that Jesus is coming soon. For example, in Matthew 24:22 Jesus declares, "If those days had not been cut short, no one would survive, but for the sake of the elect those days will be shortened."

Throughout most of our world's history such an idea would have seemed preposterous. How could life on the whole planet come to an end? People might be able to do quite a bit of damage, but to bring all human life to an end—that would be impossible! But today we actually have the capacity, with just the push of a couple buttons, to terminate all life. And if the past is any guide, we have never been good at restraint from using the power at our disposal. We live in a time when human life on our planet faces great threats. Thus it would be foolish to fail to see the significance of the time in which we live. I believe Jesus is coming soon. But it is not the time of His return that should motivate us to live faithfully for Him—it is who He is and what He has done for us.

How to Survive Armageddon

So while Jesus never answers the disciples' "when" question, we do see evidence in our world that the time is very soon. Another of Jesus' statements in Matthew 24 tells us that the gospel would be preached to the whole world before He returned (verse 14). Today we have the capacity to spread the gospel with communication media that no one would have dreamed of only a generation ago. That is another indication that we are living in the last part of the final days. In the next chapter we look at a passage in the book of Revelation that gives us more detail about what it means for the gospel to be preached to the whole world as preparation for the return of Jesus.

Chapter 10
THREE ANGELS AND THE MARK OF THE BEAST

Jesus said that the gospel of the kingdom would be preached to the whole world (Matthew 24:14). In Revelation 14 John sees a vision about three angels who proclaim this gospel to prepare the world for the return of Jesus. The passage shows us what is crucial about the gospel and why it is so important that it reach the whole world. The messages of the three angels appear in Revelation 14:6-12:

"Then I saw another angel flying in midair, and he had the eternal gospel to proclaim to those who live on the earth—to every nation, tribe, language and people. He said in a loud voice, 'Fear God and give him glory, because the hour of his judgment has come. Worship him who made the heavens, the earth, the sea and the springs of water.'

"A second angel followed and said, '"Fallen! Fallen is Babylon the Great," which made all the nations drink the maddening wine of her adulteries.'

"A third angel followed them and said in a loud voice: 'If anyone worships the beast and its image and receives its mark on their forehead or on their hand, they, too, will drink the wine of God's fury, which has been poured full strength into the cup of his wrath. They will be tormented with burning sulfur in the presence of the holy angels and of the Lamb. And the smoke of their torment will rise for ever and ever. There will be no rest day or night for those who worship the beast and its image, or for anyone who receives the mark of its name.' This calls for patient endurance on the part of the people of God who keep his commands and remain faithful to Jesus."

The first angel proclaims the eternal gospel to all who live on earth. The fact that his message is both eternal and is the "gospel" is significant for several reasons. First, it shows that the gospel doesn't change. It is the same from beginning to end. There is only one gospel. God's message of salvation is the same in the Old and New Testaments. Second, the very word "gospel" means "good news." We need to remember that God's message, including all that He tells us about the end of the world, is good news.

Let's flesh this out a little. The good news is that we are saved not by our good works but by God's grace, which is revealed in Jesus Christ. The Second Coming is a part of salvation by grace. So God's final message to the world is not bad news—it is good news. The fact that it is eternal good news shows that it is the same story of grace that God has been revealing to His people from the beginning. True, we saw its fullness only when Jesus came. But even before then, humanity was still saved by God's grace. Some have the mistaken view that God had one way of saving people in the Old Testament and another way once Jesus came. At one time people's works brought them salvation. They were saved by keeping the law. But now, some claim, all that has changed.

Paul, however, shows in Romans 4 that Abraham was saved by faith. He had not, of course, been aware of what Jesus Christ would do when He entered the world, but he trusted God's promise that He would provide for salvation, and that trust in God was Abraham's salvation. The only message of salvation throughout the Bible is trust in God and His saving grace. That is why it is so important to see that the first angel has the "eternal gospel" to proclaim to those living on earth. The message of the end-time is not new. It may come with a new sense of urgency, but it is the everlasting gospel.

This proclamation of the eternal gospel is the fulfillment of Matthew 24:14 and prepares the way for Jesus to return. It also shows us what is crucial for humans to do to in response to such good news and thus prepare themselves for the return of Jesus. It involves our *worship*. We are called to fear or reverence God, give Him glory, and worship Him. When we understand what God has done for us, the only possible appropriate response is worship.

Have you ever noticed how we tend to praise whatever we appreciate or whatever excites us. When you see a friend who has a new car or a new cell phone, don't be surprised if you listen to some words of praise. And as we truly grasp the enormity of God's grace for us, the only appropriate response is praise and worship. Therefore the message of the eternal gospel is inevitably followed by praise.

To worship anything but the true God is to worship an idol, for only God is worthy of worship. As God judges the world in preparation for the return of

How to Survive Armageddon

His Son, He summons all people of the earth to worship the true God. This message of the coming kingdom knows no limits or distinctions among humanity. It is for every nation, every race, every language group, and every culture. All are called to worship the only true God. He is the creator of all that is. Thus the good news of salvation through God's grace is made even better news by the fact that it includes everyone.

The second angel speaks of a false system of worship, Babylon. In the Old Testament Babylon was the enemy of God's people. It destroyed their Temple and carried them into captivity. Therefore Babylon represents those values opposed to God and His people. Revelation 18 explains the statement about the fall of Babylon in detail. In that chapter funeral dirges are sung for Babylon, a stark contrast to the hymns offered throughout Revelation in praise of God.

What is so bad about Babylon? In Revelation 18 we find that its way of life is one of luxury, greed, and oppression. Verse 5 tells us that her sins are piled up to heaven, yet she does not mourn or recognize what she has done. So what did she do? For one thing, she accumulated wealth for herself at the expense of others. She dealt in all kinds of commodities, from gold and silver to fine linen and delicious delicacies (verses 11-13). But worst of all, she traded in the commodity of selling human beings as slaves. Babylon treated people as if they were things (verse 13). In addition, she was interested in power and status. Thus the kings of the earth mourn over her fall as well (verse 9).

What the second angel of Revelation 14 is saying is that the whole system of values that concentrates on greed, luxury, power, status, violence, and oppression represented by Babylon is a sinking ship. It may look like it rules, but it is opposed to God's kingdom, and His kingdom will ultimately triumph. So Babylon may look powerful and attractive, but it cannot endure. Get out of it because its collapse is inevitable. Babylon is going down.

The third angel warns against worshipping the beast and its image rather than worshipping the true God. In other words, Satan has a false system of worship to draw people away from the true God. In order to understand this beast, we need to go back to Revelation 12. There we find a dragon. At one time the dragon was in heaven, caused war in heaven, and was thrown to the earth, where it tried to kill the One who was born into the world and will one day rule it, clearly a reference to Jesus. Revelation 12:9 clearly identifies this dragon: "The great dragon was hurled down—that ancient serpent called the devil, or Satan, who leads the whole world astray. He was hurled to the earth, and his angels with him."

When we come to Revelation 13, we find that the dragon, Satan, works through other entities as well. In verses 1-4 we encounter both a beast and an image to that beast with whom he shares his power.

"The dragon stood on the shore of the sea. And I saw a beast coming out of the sea. It had ten horns and seven heads, with ten crowns on its horns, and on each head a blasphemous name. The beast I saw resembled a leopard, but had feet like those of a bear and a mouth like that of a lion. The dragon gave the beast his power and his throne and great authority. One of the heads of the beast seemed to have had a fatal wound, but the fatal wound had been healed. The whole world was filled with wonder and followed the beast. People worshiped the dragon because he had given authority to the beast, and they also worshiped the beast and asked, 'Who is like the beast? Who can wage war against it?'"

In other words, Satan uses political and religious agencies in our world to carry out his purpose and to try to entice people away from worshipping the Creator God. The second beast, who is an image to the first beast, enforces the demands of the first beast to be worshipped. The issue again is worship. Whom will we worship—the true God, or the dragon and the earthly powers through which he works?

How do we know the difference? In the third angel's message we see clearly that the ones faithful to God and who worship Him are those who obey His commandments and are faithful to Jesus (Revelation 14:12). They keep His commandments, not in order to be saved, but because they are saved. In fact, that was always God's intention for the commandments. When you look at the giving of the Ten Commandments in Exodus 20, they begin with an affirmation that God has already taken the initiative to save His people. He announced, "I am the Lord your God, who brought you out of Egypt, out of the land of slavery" (verse 2).

God's liberating His people from slavery in Egypt was the great symbol of His saving grace in the Old Testament. The Lord never intended people to earn their salvation through obedience to the commandments. Keeping the commandments was their response to His saving grace.

So in the end, God's people will be those who are so grateful for His salvation that they will respond by worshipping Him, following His commandments, and being faithful to Jesus. To receive the mark of the beast is to allow the beast to substitute the true worship of faith in God and obedience to His commandments with another false object of worship. The mark is depicted as being in the forehead and hand, probably referring to the allegiance given to the beast in both thought and action.

Two interesting references in the messages of these angels allude to one of God's commandments that the Christian world today often neglects. The language in the description of the true Creator God who is to be worshipped ("Worship him who made the heavens, the earth, the sea and the springs of water") comes from the fourth commandment of the Ten Commandments that we find in Exodus 20:8-11:

"Remember the Sabbath day by keeping it holy. Six days you shall labor and do all your work, but the seventh day is a sabbath to the Lord your God. On it you shall not do any work, neither you, nor your son or daughter, nor your male or female servant, nor your animals, nor any foreigner residing in your towns. For in six days *the Lord made the heavens and the earth, the sea, and all that is in them,* but he rested on the seventh day. Therefore the Lord blessed the Sabbath day and made it holy."

The second reference is in Revelation 14:11. It tells us that there is no rest for those who worship the beast and his image. The Sabbath command asks us to remember God as Creator and to rest in remembrance of His creation. Thus Revelation seems to bring special attention to the Sabbath command as one that keeps God's people focused on worshipping the one true God. But the beast tries to turn attention away from the Creator God and His invitation for His people to rest in Him.

Therefore one of the most important of the last-day events we need to know about is the attempt by the beast to lead us away from the worship of the true Creator God. Can we identify the beast and know for sure who it is? Perhaps more important than giving the beast a specific identity is seeing what the issues are in the beast's existence and activity. It may be that at different times Satan works through different entities. It is hard to imagine that in John's day, when the members of the seven churches outlined in chapters 2 and 3 first heard the book of Revelation, that they would not have thought of pagan Rome as the beast. Rome was trying to get them to turn away from God and bow to the emperor and his image. We know that at least one person in the church at Pergamum (see Revelation 2:13) had suffered martyrdom for faithfulness to Christ at the hands of the Roman government. But of course, Pagan Rome is no longer here. What powers might be trying to turn us away from true worship and obedience to God's commandments now?

I was teaching a class on the book of Revelation many years ago and was setting forth my ideas on the identity of the beast when a student toward the back of the classroom raised his hand and said, "I think in my country we faced the beast." I asked him to explain. He told me that in the African country where he lived a regime hostile to Christianity had ruled and demanded that people renounce their faith and worship the new leader of the country instead. Soldiers went from door to door and ordered people to bow to a statue of their leader and give him worship or they would be put to death. Some of his relatives had been killed. What should I have told him? Should I have said, "No, you didn't face the beast—the beast is something quite different"?

I must confess that I didn't say that. It seems that the issues of the struggle between Christ and Satan outlined here in Revelation 14 are exactly those that he and his family had faced in their country. Maybe we should say, "If the shoe fits, wear it." We certainly seem to see the evidence of the dragon's power in what he faced.

But that does not mean that we can go around accusing anybody we don't like of being the beast. Scripture presents some clear specifications here. The beast tries to entice people into false worship instead of worshipping the true Creator God, and seeks to force people to disobey God's law. It uses the threat of death to undermine obedience to divine law and faithfulness to Jesus.

The good news is that no one has to receive the mark of the beast. In fact, we don't really have to worry about the beast if we keep our eyes fixed on worshipping the one true God, being faithful to Christ and His message, and keeping God's commandments (all 10 of them, including the invitation to remember God on the Sabbath day). That is the profile of those who are the people of God. When we are focused on God, Satan and His beast have no power over us.

In our hustle-bustle society it is easy to neglect the very thing that these angels call for in preparation for Christ's return, which is worship. The crucial issue in our lives is who we worship. The book of Hebrews warns us about the danger of neglecting worship together with others.

"Let us hold unswervingly to the hope we profess, for he who promised is faithful. And let us consider how we may spur one another on toward love and good deeds, not giving up meeting together, as some are in the habit of doing, but encouraging one another—and all the more as you see the Day approaching" (Hebrews 10:23-25).

Our safety in being prepared for the return of Christ has to do with our worship. It is important to be part of a worshipping community that keeps the commandments of God and remains faithful to Jesus.

A few months ago I talked with a woman who had had a terrible week. She had gone to the doctor for a biopsy, and it had come back with a diagnosis of cancer. Devastated, she decided not to go to church. Unhappy with God, she didn't want to have to see others. And besides, she didn't really have anything to wear.

Yet deep down inside she felt the need to be with God's people and join in worshipping Him. When the time came, she realized she did have something to wear. That had been just an excuse. During the prayer at church, when those with special requests were invited forward, she went to the front. Her silent prayer was that God would take away her fear. Never, she told me, was a prayer answered so quickly. Then she heard a testimony from another person who had gone through an experience similar to hers. Now the woman even entered into the singing of the hymn of praise to God, something that until that moment she didn't think she could do with the heavy heart she had. Afterward she went home grateful for the privilege of worship, and with the feeling that a huge burden had been taken off her shoulders.

As we draw toward the end of our world's history, God invites us to worship Him. When we do, we will not have to worry about the mark of the beast, but will be among the people of God who obey His commandments and remain faithful to Jesus.

CHAPTER 11
PESTILENCE, PERSECUTION, AND PLAGUES

Throughout this book we have emphasized that the subject of the promised return of Jesus, which we find permeating the New Testament, is a matter of joyful hope. God's people look forward to Christ's return. Yet I'm sure some might be wondering, *Are you really telling us the whole story? When I look at the Bible, I find all kinds of scary things about the Second Coming and the events leading up to it. Aren't there reasons for fear and trauma rather than joy and hope?*

Those who ask such a question might have a point. After all, we do find references to pestilence, persecution, and plagues in the Bible as well. For example, when Jesus talks to His disciples about His return in Matthew 24, a chapter we have looked at several times, He warns them that they will encounter persecution. Here is what He says in Matthew 24:9: "Then you will be handed over to be persecuted and put to death, and you will be hated by all nations because of me."

Somehow that doesn't sound too joyous or hopeful, does it? Nobody really wants to be hated and persecuted. But it gets even worse when we go to the book of Revelation. In chapters 6 and 7 we read about the opening of some seals that leads to a number of catastrophes. In the fourth seal the prophecy sounds particularly ominous.

"When the Lamb opened the fourth seal, I heard the voice of the fourth living creature say, 'Come!' I looked, and there before me was a pale horse! Its rider was named Death, and Hades was following close behind him. They were given power over a fourth of the earth to kill by sword, famine and plague, and by the wild beasts of the earth" (Revelation 6:7, 8).

The death of one fourth of humanity is particularly disturbing. But when Revelation talks about the seven trumpets in chapters 8 and 9 it gets even more frightening. Notice the peril of the fifth trumpet (also called the "first woe").

"And the agony they suffered was like that of the sting of a scorpion when it strikes. During those days people will seek death but will not find it; they will long to die, but death will elude them" (Revelation 9:5).

Then in the sixth trumpet (the "second woe") a third of the human race perishes.

"The horses and riders I saw in my vision looked like this: Their breastplates were fiery red, dark blue, and yellow as sulfur. The heads of the horses resembled the heads of lions, and out of their mouths came fire, smoke and sulfur. A third of mankind was killed by the three plagues of fire, smoke and sulfur that came out of their mouths. The power of the horses was in their mouths and in their tails; for their tails were like snakes, having heads with which they inflict injury" (verses 17-19).

Does this sound like joyful hope? But it gets even worse. As we move on in the book of Revelation to chapter 16 we encounter the seven plagues, which even surpass the seven seals and seven trumpets in their destruction and terror. When the angels pour out the seven plagues on the earth the following occur:

1. Sores afflict human beings.
2. The sea is turned to blood.
3. The rivers and springs are turned to blood.
4. The sun scorches the earth with fire.
5. Darkness occurs on the earth.
6. The river Euphrates dries up to prepare the way for the battle of Armageddon.
7. Lightning, thunder, earthquakes, and hail bring trauma to the earth.

We see how terrible the hail is in Revelation 16:21: "From the sky huge hailstones, each weighing about a hundred pounds, fell on people. And they cursed God on account of the plague of hail, because the plague was so terrible."

The thought of hailstones weighing 100 pounds each is not exactly a cheerful one! How then can we emphasize the joy and hope of the Second Coming when pestilence, persecution, and plagues seem more likely to evoke panic? Is the topic of the second coming of Jesus more about pestilence and plagues than about promise?

Let me give you five reasons we can be hopeful about the future and about the return of Jesus in spite of the fact that we do find mention of pestilence, persecution, and plagues in the Bible. All five reasons come from the Bible. Let's take a look.

1. God promises to be with us.

It is true that Jesus told His disciples they would face persecution. But He also promised that He would be with them, through the Holy Spirit, when they endured it. They would not be left alone. In Mark 13:11 He promises them that "whenever you are arrested and brought to trial, do not worry beforehand about what to say. Just say whatever is given you at the time, for it is not you speaking, but the Holy Spirit."

Jesus' disciples may be oppressed and arrested, but they are not abandoned. They don't even need to worry what to say in such situations, for the Holy Spirit will be with them to guide and direct. That should comfort us when we fear the persecution of the last days.

2. Before the description of the plagues we find a great song of victory.

The seven last plagues, the epitome of hard times on the earth, occur in Revelation 16. But chapter 15 depicts singing. It is of victory and deliverance. You see, several times a vision of God's already victorious people around the throne will suddenly interrupt the flow of the book of Revelation. Such visions are not chronological, for they recur throughout the book. The idea is that at crucial points John lifts the veil of heaven to show his readers their final destiny. That destiny is to surround the throne of God and sing praises for the great victory of eternal life that He has given them. It is significant that one of those periodic visions of victory and singing comes just before the plagues are poured out on the earth. Look at the joy and sense of triumph in Revelation 15:1-4.

"I saw in heaven another great and marvelous sign: seven angels with the seven last plagues—last, because with them God's wrath is completed. And I saw what looked like a sea of glass glowing with fire and, standing beside the sea, those who had been victorious over the beast and its image and over the number of its name. They held harps given them by God and sang the song of God's servant Moses and of the Lamb:

> 'Great and marvelous are your deeds,
>> Lord God Almighty.
> Just and true are your ways,
>> King of the nations.
> Who will not fear you, Lord,
>> and bring glory to your name?
> For you alone are holy.
> All nations will come
>> and worship before you,
>> for your righteous acts have been revealed.'"

Why joyful singing before something so terrible as the seven last plagues? It doesn't seem logical. Yet to John it made perfectly good sense. We find singing associated with the plagues that we find in the Old Testament book of Exodus. Pharaoh, the Egyptian ruler, was oppressing God's people, enslaving them and forcing them into tortuous hard labor. The Lord told him to let His people go. But Pharaoh refused again and again. Finally God sent a series of 10 plagues to help convince Pharaoh to free the Israelites. But Pharaoh still refused. The 10 plagues have similarities to the seven last plagues we see in Revelation, but they are not identical. The 10 plagues of Exodus were:

1. The Nile River turned to blood
2. Frogs
3. Gnats
4. Flies

5. The livestock killed
6. Boils
7. Hail
8. Locusts
9. Darkness
10. Death of the firstborn

Finally Pharaoh let the people leave, only to change his mind and pursue them. When it looked as if they were trapped, God opened the Red Sea, and they walked through safely, whereas the water swallowed Pharaoh and his pursuing troops when they tried to follow.

After the victory for God's people, Moses led them in singing the song of Moses. We find it in Exodus 15. Here are just the first four verses of it:

"I will sing to the Lord,
   for he is highly exalted.
Both horse and driver
   he has hurled into the sea.
The Lord is my strength and my defense;
   he has become my salvation.
He is my God, and I will praise him,
   my father's God, and I will exalt him.
The Lord is a warrior;
   the Lord is his name.
Pharaoh's chariots and his army
   he has hurled into the sea."

As you can see, it is a song of victory. God has rescued His people. According to Revelation 15 the people around God's throne sing the song of Moses, one of triumph. But it is not only the song of Moses. It is also the song of the Lamb, the Lamb who takes away the sin of the world, the Lamb who is worthy of praise. But we notice still another difference. Israel sang the song of Moses *after* the plagues and their deliverance. The song of Moses and the Lamb is sung *before* the seven last plagues, for Jesus' death and resurrection makes the final victory of God's people so sure that the song can be sung in advance. The plagues in Revelation, as they were in Exodus, are a prelude to the deliverance of God's people. We can be hopeful in spite of plagues because even before they strike, God's people receive assurance of victory and can see the vision of their ultimate destiny with God. If the courts of heaven can sing for joy before the plagues, shouldn't we be able to have joyful hope in spite of them?

3. The plagues fall on the wicked.

Look at what the book of Revelation says about the first plague in Revelation 16:2:

"The first angel went and poured out his bowl on the land, and ugly, festering sores broke out on the people who had the mark of the beast and worshiped its image."

During the Exodus the plagues fell on Pharaoh and his followers. So in Revelation the plagues strike those who have the mark of the beast and worship its image. We have already seen that we need not receive the mark of the beast, and so we don't have to worry about the plagues. God will be watching over His people. Certainly that doesn't mean Christians will escape suffering, just as they are not free from the suffering that afflicts the world now. But God is with them and will watch over them. We notice again in the third plague that it is those who have opposed God's people and shed their blood who receive the blood to drink:

Pestilence, Persecution, and Plagues

"You are just in these judgments, O Holy One,
    you who are and who were;
  for they have shed the blood of your holy
      people and your prophets,
    and you have given them blood to drink as
      they deserve" (verses 5, 6).

The plague is connected to their sin. They shed the blood of God's people, and now it comes back to haunt them. The wicked now drink blood. It is what they deserve. The original text says they are "worthy," an obvious contrast with the Lamb in Revelation 5, who is worthy of praise. Thus He is worthy of praise, and they are worthy to drink blood.

Yet even here God's goal is to bring about the repentance of those who receive the plagues, just as He tried to convince Pharaoh through the plagues of old. Yet as did Pharaoh, the wicked refuse to repent, as we see in the fourth plague.

"The fourth angel poured out his bowl on the sun, and the sun was allowed to scorch people with fire. They were seared by the intense heat and they cursed the name of God, who had control over these plagues, but they refused to repent and glorify him" (verses 8, 9).

God is doing all He can to bring everyone to repentance, but some are unwilling. However, we do not need to panic about the plagues if we turn to God and glorify Him. Does it mean that God is good only to those who serve Him and pours out His wrath on everyone else? If understood properly, even God's wrath gives us reason for hope. That brings us to our fourth reason we can be joyful and hopeful in spite of pestilence, persecution, and plagues.

4. God's wrath is the other side of His love.

John tells us in Revelation 15:1 that the plagues are called the "last" plagues because with them the "wrath" of God comes to an end. Divine wrath certainly sounds like a scary idea! How can we avoid fear and panic about the future plagues when they represent divine wrath?

When we study God's wrath in the Bible we find that it takes two forms. On the one hand, it is His action against the oppressor in favor of the oppressed. Think again of the exodus from Egypt. If Pharaoh insisted on enslaving and torturing God's people, and the Lord loved His people and wanted them rescued, then He had to do something about Pharaoh. Divine wrath in this case is the other side of His rescuing and delivering love. We see it in what He does for the oppressed.

The other form of God's wrath is His giving people over to the consequences of their own decisions. It is the reverse side of His principle of freedom. God never forces anyone but gives them the liberty to choose. But such freedom, however, has consequences. It would not be true freedom if God didn't allow us to carry through with the inevitable results of our decisions. So when Paul sets forth what he calls the revelation of God's wrath in Romans 1:18, he defines it in terms of God giving people over to their own choices. He repeats the expression three times in Romans 1. In the third case he says:

"Furthermore, just as they did not think it worthwhile to retain the knowledge of God, so *God gave them over* to a depraved mind, so that they do what ought not to be done. They have become filled with every kind of wickedness, evil, greed and depravity. They are full of envy, murder, strife, deceit and malice" (verses 28, 29).

God values freedom so much that He permits people to receive the consequences of their own decisions. But even then His wrath is not the last word. God gave the sinners over to their sinful decisions, but He then gave Christ over to be their Savior. (Romans 8:32 uses the same word for Christ being delivered over to save us as Romans 1:28 employs for God handing sinners over.)

Therefore God's wrath is really the other side of His loving desire to honor freedom and to rescue us from oppression. Thus even divine wrath is not reason for fear and panic. It should lead us to see how gracious God is as we come to Him for rescue and salvation.

But there is still one more reason we can be hopeful in spite of pestilence, persecution, and plagues.

5. Even God's judgment is good news.

As we already saw under reason 2, in which we introduced the song of Moses and the Lamb, the whole thrust of the plagues is to show that God is just and fair in everything. He is faithful and loving in what He does for every human being, including His judgments.

> "You are just in these judgments, O Holy One,
>   you who are and who were. . . .
> "Yes, Lord God Almighty,
>   true and just are your judgments" (Revelation 16:5-7).

Through the entire sweep of God's interaction with His world and His people He has been only loving, faithful, and fair. It is true that the book of Revelation presents a picture of increasing difficulty and disaster on the earth as we move through the seals, trumpets, and plagues. But whatever God does, it has one purpose in mind: to save everyone who will allow Him to redeem them. His goal is to have mercy on everyone, as Paul shows in Romans 11:32: "For God has bound everyone over to disobedience so that he may have mercy on them all."

God's whole purpose is to save. If we keep our eyes focused on Christ and His promise, this good news gives us assurance and hope. We don't need to fear the judgment. Remember what we saw earlier in chapter 5, "Eternal Life Now." If we are in Christ, we have already passed from death to life and have already been judged. God's judgment is good news, because it means that He will bring an end to all the problems that sin has brought. Pestilence, persecution, and plagues give way to new heaven and new earth, as we will see in the next chapter.

For this reason the thought of God's judgment should not only be free of fear and panic—it should be something that we look forward to. It should bring us great joy that in the end it is not the problems and plagues that have the last word, but it is God's faithful and fair judgments that prevail. That is why in Psalm 96 we see a picture of rejoicing about judgment. The psalmist calls for singing and rejoicing because God comes to judge. And this rejoicing erupts not only from humans but from the entire world. All of nature joins in praising God for His judgment.

> "Worship the Lord in the splendor of his holiness;
> tremble before him, all the earth.
> Say among the nations, 'The Lord reigns.'

> The world is firmly established, it cannot be
>   moved;
>   he will judge the peoples with equity.
> Let the heavens rejoice, let the earth be glad;
>   let the sea resound, and all that is in it.
> Let the fields be jubilant, and everything in
>   them;
>   let all the trees of the forest sing for joy.
> Let all creation rejoice before the Lord, for
>   he comes,
>   he comes to judge the earth.
> He will judge the world in righteousness
>   and the peoples in his faithfulness" (Psalm
>   96:9-13).

What rejoicing from the whole of creation! Even judgment is good news. Pestilence, persecution, and plagues are no reason for panic, for our real focus should be on the great promise of salvation.

When my son was in the first grade, he was quite sure he had good reason for panic. As he came in from recess one day, his teacher informed him that the principal wanted him in his office. Now, when you are in the first grade, it is scary enough to have to go to the principal's office. That long walk down the hall to the ominous office puts panic into the heart of any child.

But to make matters worse, my son knew exactly why he was being called to the principal's office, and he knew that he was guilty. During recess he had gotten into a dirt clod fight with another student. He was pretty sure that's why the principal wanted to see him.

To make matters worse, he had heard the stories the upper graders told the first graders about the paddle that hung on the wall of the principal's office. It was no ordinary paddle. It had nails driven through it, and if you were called into the principal's office you would feel its terror.

But even more frightening, the boy he had gotten into the dirt clod fight with was the principal's son! It was a pretty scared kid who entered that office. The first thing he did was look around to find the paddle on the wall. It wasn't there. Instead of the wrath he expected, the principal smiled and said, "Larry, I like you, and I really wouldn't want you to get hurt. I'm afraid you might when dirt clods are flying through the air. Do you think you could get by without having dirt clod fights? I thought you could. Go have a good day."

My son left with a wide smile and a wider sigh of relief. Instead of the wrath he expected, he had found love and grace.

It is the same with God. Even His judgment is good news. We can join the whole world in its joyful hope as we sing:

"Let all creation rejoice before the Lord, for he comes, he comes to judge the earth. He will judge the world in righteousness and the peoples in his faithfulness."

CHAPTER 12
AFTER JESUS COMES

M uch of what we have seen so far has to do with the time before Jesus comes. What will happen? How are we to live? In this chapter we focus on what takes place after Jesus returns. First a brief review, however, of what transpires before the second coming of Christ.

We have seen that the world will become worse leading up to the second advent of Christ. A series of plagues will bring disaster and catastrophe. God, however, continues to watch over His people. And history continues on right up to the end. As Jesus said, people would be going about their regular round of duties, just as at the time of the Flood people were eating, drinking, and marrying off their children, unaware of the coming disaster. Look at what Jesus says in Matthew 24:37-39:

"As it was in the days of Noah, so it will be at the coming of the Son of Man. For in the days before the flood, people were eating and drinking, marrying and giving in marriage, up to the day Noah entered the ark; and they knew nothing about what would happen until the flood came and took them all away. That is how it will be at the coming of the Son of Man."

In other words, people will be going to work, buying stocks, selling houses, sending their kids off to school, getting ready for weddings, talking with

How to Survive Armageddon

Facebook friends, and a myriad of other daily activities right up until the time Jesus arrives. They will not be expecting anything out of the usual.

But the unusual will happen all of a sudden. Jesus will appear in the clouds of heaven in a visible, audible way for all to see. It will be like lightning flashing from horizon to horizon, and every eye will see Him. The voice of the archangel will call out, and the trumpet will sound. As Jesus hovers above the earth, the graves will spring open and all who have trusted in God for their salvation will come forth from the tomb. It is actually an act of re-creation. God summons these people to life and transforms them so that they now have a new body like that of Christ, no longer subject to death. As Paul says in Philippians 3:20, 21:

"But our citizenship is in heaven. And we eagerly await a Savior from there, the Lord Jesus Christ, who, by the power that enables him to bring everything under his control, will transform our lowly bodies so that they will be like his glorious body."

This new and glorious body is now immortal or imperishable as Paul shows in 1 Corinthians 15:51-54:

"Listen, I tell you a mystery: We will not all sleep, but we will all be changed—in a flash, in the twinkling of an eye, at the last trumpet. For the trumpet will sound, the dead will be raised imperishable, and we will be changed. For the perishable must clothe itself with the imperishable, and the mortal with immortality. When the perishable has been clothed with the imperishable, and the mortal with immortality, then the saying that is written will come true: 'Death has been swallowed up in victory.'"

The transformation occurs not only for the dead raised at this time, but for the righteous still alive when Christ comes. They too will receive an immortal and imperishable body. Then they are caught up into the clouds along with the resurrected, and both groups join Christ to be with Him forever, as we see in 1 Thessalonians 4:15-17:

"According to the Lord's word, we tell you that we who are still alive, who are left until the coming of the Lord, will certainly not precede those who have fallen asleep. For the Lord himself will come down from heaven, with a loud command, with the voice of the archangel and with the trumpet call of God, and the dead in Christ will rise first. After that, we who are still alive and are left will be caught up together with them in the clouds to meet the Lord in the air. And so we will be with the Lord forever."

In order to discover what happens after the Second Coming, we need to turn to the book of Revelation, especially the last three chapters. In Revelation 20:4 we hear about the group we have just noticed, the righteous dead resurrected and gathered to be with Christ forever, and the living righteous who accompany them. Apparently they are allowed to see God's work of judgment and affirm that God has been fair and true in all His dealings with women and men. Revelation 20:4-6 declares:

"I saw thrones on which were seated those who had been given authority to judge. And I saw the souls of those who had been beheaded because of their testimony about Jesus and because of the word of God. They had not worshiped the beast or its image and had not received its mark on their foreheads or their hands. They came to life and reigned with Christ a thousand years. (The rest of the dead did not come to life until the thousand years were ended.) This is the first resurrection. Blessed and holy are those who share in the first resurrection. The second death has no power over them, but they will be priests of God and of Christ and will reign with him for a thousand years."

The redeemed of all ages join Christ in heaven and live and reign with Him there 1,000 years. During this time they receive authority to review God's work of judgment to confirm that it has been fair and just in every way. They belong to the first resurrection. The second death, which refers to the final death, will have no power over them. Their deaths on earth have been only a temporary sleep from which God awakened them with the angel's shout and the trumpet call. Transformed, they are now immune to death.

But the passage also refers to another group—"the rest of the dead." They are different from the righteous dead, and must therefore be the wicked dead. They do not live until the 1,000 years have concluded, and thus were not resurrected at the second coming of Jesus. Instead, they simply continued to sleep during that period and did not receive the blessing pronounced on the first group. So for 1,000 years the righteous dwell in heaven with Christ and the wicked remain in their state of death.

Where is Satan during this time? He finds himself chained, because he has no one to tempt. The righteous are in heaven and the wicked are dead. And he is left in an abyss to think over what he has done, as we read in Revelation 20:1-3:

"And I saw an angel coming down out of heaven, having the key to the Abyss and holding in his hand a great chain. He seized the dragon, that ancient serpent, who is the devil, or Satan, and bound him for a thousand years. He threw him into the Abyss, and locked and sealed it over him, to keep him from deceiving the nations anymore until the thousand years were ended. After that, he must be set free for a short time."

The devil is simply bound for 1,000 years with no one to deceive. But at the end of that period our text says that he will be released for a short time. In order to see what this is all about, we need to make an important inference from verse 5 and then go down to verse 7 of Revelation 20. As you see in the translation that we are using, verse 5 is a parenthetical statement. It announces that the rest of the dead—that is, the wicked—did not live again until the 1,000 years concluded, implying a resurrection of the wicked at its end. They come to life again and live on the earth, even as the righteous are in heaven.

According to verse 7, this presents the devil with another opportunity to seduce his followers. He seeks to organize the wicked to defeat God and His people.

"When the thousand years are over, Satan will be released from his prison and will go out to deceive the nations in the four corners of the earth—Gog and Magog—and to gather them for battle. In number they are like the sand on the seashore. They marched across the breadth of the earth and surrounded the camp of God's people, the city he loves. But fire came down from heaven and devoured them" (verses 7-9).

"Gog and Magog" comes from Ezekiel 38 and

How to Survive Armageddon

39. Here in Revelation it refers to this final battle in which Satan and the wicked, after their resurrection at the end of the 1,000 years, try to seize God's city as it descends to earth. But fire devours and totally annihilates them. According to verse 14, this is now the second death. From it there is no resurrection. It is a final death that brings sin to an end. While it is, of course, not God's will that any should suffer the second death, He still respects the freedom of those who desire not to be part of His kingdom. They have chosen to reject God, and since He is the source of life, they have forfeited life forever.

It is at this point, after the 1,000 years, that God brings the home of the redeemed from heaven back to this earth. It was always His intent to restore life on our world to what He intended it to be before sin entered and marred its perfection. After the final failure of Satan and his forces, God re-creates our world.

"Then I saw 'a new heaven and a new earth,' for the first heaven and the first earth had passed away, and there was no longer any sea. I saw the Holy City, the new Jerusalem, coming down out of heaven from God, prepared as a bride beautifully dressed for her husband. And I heard a loud voice from the throne saying, 'Look! God's dwelling place is now among the people, and he will dwell with them. They will be his people, and God himself will be with them and be their God. "He will wipe every tear from their eyes. There will be no more death" or mourning or crying or pain, for the old order of things has passed away.'

"He who was seated on the throne said, 'I am making everything new!' Then he said, 'Write this down, for these words are trustworthy and true'" (Revelation 21:1-5).

Imagine a world with no pain, no crying, no death. It is what God is preparing for His people. After the end of the 1,000 years such a world will go on forever. Never again will sin rise to destroy the beauty of God's order. For all eternity the redeemed will be with Him—He will be their God, and they will be His people. Thus we see that the final hope of salvation is not escape from the earth, but living in a renewed one. It is not living without a body, but living with a new and glorious one. Nor is it ethereal existence in a spirit world, but life lived on this earth as God originally intended. Christian hope is not pie in the sky by and by, but the restoration of all that is good about the life God created for us at the beginning.

Those who live in God's city will eat of the tree of life and drink freely of the water of life (see Revelation 22). And the best news is that we are all invited. All this can be ours. God wants it to be ours. All we need to do is put our trust in Him and accept the invitation we find in Revelation 22:17: "The Spirit and the bride say, 'Come!' And let the one who hears say, 'Come!' Let the one who is thirsty come; and let the one who wishes take the free gift of the water of life."

CHAPTER 13
LIVING THE KINGDOM

For my wife and me nothing is better than having both our kids and all three of our grandkids visit us at the same time. We always try to make those rare moments extra-special. One day we took the boys to Disneyland, also known as the Magic Kingdom, for them to have a good time. Two of the three boys did, but one grandson, who is usually the happiest of the three, had a bad day. It started even before we got into the park. When we paused to take a picture of the whole clan before we went through the gate, he didn't want to stop. In the picture everyone is smiling but him, and he is crying. It wasn't long after we reached Disneyland that he decided he was hungry and needed to eat. While one grandson went on the merry-go-round and had a great time, and another enjoyed the Mister Toad ride (even though he thought it was a bit scary), the third grandson didn't go on anything. He made his mom get him some food.

By the time the rest of us wanted lunch, he wasn't hungry anymore. He couldn't understand why he had to go into the restaurant with us since we were the only hungry ones. The day went downhill from there. When we left for home in the evening, two of the grandsons had had a great day, but one was fussing and unhappy. At the breakfast table the next day the one who had been unhappy the day before said, "We need to go to Disneyland again. I didn't have much fun. I was just too grumpy." No one disagreed.

You see, three boys went to the Magic Kingdom that day, but only two of them had the spirit of the Magic Kingdom in their hearts. The other one never really enjoyed it because the spirit of the kingdom wasn't in him.

During the time Jesus was on earth He talked a lot about His kingdom. We know that the kingdom of God will fully come only in the future. In Matthew 24:14 Jesus declares, "And this gospel of the kingdom will be preached in the whole world as a testimony to all nations, and then the end will come."

When Jesus instituted the Lord's Supper for the disciples, He made the kingdom sound future. "After taking the cup, he gave thanks and said, 'Take this and divide it among you. For I tell you I will not drink again from the fruit of the vine until the kingdom of God comes'" (Luke 22:17, 18).

One day, however, the Pharisees asked Him a question about the kingdom. They wanted to know when it would start. The answer Jesus gave was intriguing indeed. We read about it in Luke 17:20, 21:

"Once, on being asked by the Pharisees when the kingdom of God would come, Jesus replied, 'The coming of the kingdom of God is not something that can be observed, nor will people say, "Here it is," or "There it is," because the kingdom of God is in your midst.'"

Jesus tells the Pharisees that His kingdom is not something that they will be able to observe or point to or put their finger on. Rather, it's already here.

How to Survive Armageddon

The Savior makes it clear that in addition to the future aspect of the kingdom that will accompany His return, it has a present element as well. Right now the kingdom is in the midst of those who have eyes to see it. Jesus is talking about the kingdom being present where people are willing to see it and live by its values now. The kingdom is both future and now.

Poet Elizabeth Barrett Browning put it this way:
"Earth's crammed with heaven,

And every common bush afire with God;

But only he who sees takes off his shoes;

The rest sit round it and pluck blackberries."[1]

The apostle Paul also shows us the present aspect of the kingdom. In Colossians 1:13, 14 he tells us what God has already done for us: "For he has rescued us from the dominion of darkness and brought us into the kingdom of the Son he loves, in whom we have redemption, the forgiveness of sins."

Notice that it is in the past tense. Even though we still live in a world of sin and death, it no longer dominates us. God has already rescued us from the dominion of darkness and brought us into the kingdom of His Son. It is a present reality. The book of Revelation helps us understand how this works. As we have already seen in a previous chapter, several times in the course of going through the visions the regular flow pauses to show the saints already singing the songs of heaven around the throne of God. When they sing them, John draws on the very hymns that Christians sang in their small house churches when they worshipped God. Therefore John draws together the future victory around the throne and the present experience of

Christian worship to indicate that when we worship God here and now, we already anticipate the victory in the new earth, when we will sing around God's throne.

John is telling us that we can begin to experience now the music of the new world. The tunes of God's music—that of His kingdom—already make their way into this world. We can already begin to hear the heavenly music when we worship God with our songs and our lives. New Testament scholar N. T. Wright puts it this way:

"Christian ethics is not about discovering what is going on in this world and getting in tune with it. It isn't a matter of doing things to earn God's favor. It is not about trying to obey dusty rulebooks from long ago and far away. It is about practicing, in the present, the tunes we shall sing in God's new world."[2]

That is how we prepare for the eternal kingdom. By playing out its tunes in our life here and now we already dwell in God's kingdom.

That means we have to ask ourselves what the tunes of the kingdom sound like. What are the themes of the music that we begin singing now to announce the kingdom and make it real? While we could list many, let's limit ourselves to just a few.

Humility and service

One day Jesus' disciples began arguing about which of them would be the greatest in the kingdom when it came. James and John were quite sure they should be the top two next to Jesus in the kingdom, and they even got their mother involved in trying to make it happen. Naturally it infuriated the other disciples, and quite an argument ensued. But Jesus turned their whole understanding of what the music of the kingdom sounded like upside down. He told them that the kingdom wasn't about sitting in a seat of honor and power. Rather, it was about humble and sacrificial service for others. In Mark 10:42-45 Jesus said:

"You know that those who are regarded as rulers of the Gentiles lord it over them, and their high officials exercise authority over them. Not so with you. Instead, whoever wants to become great among you must be your servant, and whoever wants to be first must be slave of all. For even the Son of Man did not come to be served, but to serve, and to give his life as a ransom for many."

Being a slave of all may not sound that appealing, but Jesus wants to make the matter clear. The kingdom isn't about power and status—it is about humble service. And this is not necessarily the way of the world in which we presently live.

As I write this it is almost election time. Every day our mailbox is full of pamphlets and brochures trying to convince us to vote for a specific candidate. But when I read them, humility doesn't seem like a very important commodity. At least I sure don't see much of it. If we are to sing the music of heaven we must begin now to live lives of humble service for others.

Generosity

God's kingdom is a government of concern for the poor. When Jesus began His ministry on earth, He gave what amounts to a mission statement of what His work would be in our world.

"The Spirit of the Lord is on me,
    because he has anointed me
    to proclaim good news to the poor" (Luke
    4:18).

Jesus' arrival was good news for the poor. His kingdom is about generosity and sharing, not greed.

One day an outstanding young man asked Jesus what he needed to do to inherit eternal life. Christ answered that he needed to keep the commandments. The man said that he had always done that ever since he was a child. Then Jesus replied that he needed to do one more thing—he should sell everything he had and give it to the poor. In response he went away sorrowful. The disciples were startled, but Jesus astounded them even more by telling them what we find recorded in Mark 10:24-27: "'Children, how hard it is to enter the kingdom of God! It is easier for a camel to go through the eye of a needle than for someone who is rich to enter the kingdom of God.'

"The disciples were even more amazed, and said to each other, 'Who then can be saved?'

"Jesus looked at them and said, 'With man this is impossible, but not with God; all things are possible with God.'"

With God it is possible to save even the rich! Yet it is difficult, because it becomes hard for the rich to be generous and giving rather than greedy. And greed has within it the seeds of its own destruction. Just look what happened on Wall Street and in the mortgage market in the United States primarily as a result of greed. To sing the music of the kingdom in this world is to live out a spirit of gracious generosity.

How to Survive Armageddon

Peace

The music of God's kingdom is all about peace. When Jesus appeared before Pilate after His arrest, He told Pilate, "My kingdom is not of this world. If it were, my servants would fight to prevent my arrest by the Jewish leaders. But now my kingdom is from another place" (John 18:36).

Jesus' kingdom is one of nonviolence in which force doesn't win the day. It is a realm in which people turn the other cheek (see Matthew 5:39), not out of weakness, but out of a strength that resists violence by refusing to seek revenge. This stops the spiral of violence so that it cannot go on escalating as inevitably happens when we retaliate.

In Beethoven's *Missa Solemnis* the fifth movement includes the words "The Lamb of God who takes away the sins of the world" and "Give us peace." When the choir starts to sing "Give us peace (*dona nobis pacem)*" the timpani thunders the sound of war, and the trumpets suggest a march to battle. But the choir continues to call for peace, and eventually the cry "give us peace" wins out and the whole orchestra and chorus ends in a great crescendo of peace. The music of the kingdom is that of peace.

Joy

The music of the kingdom is also that of joy. When Paul wrote his letter to the Romans, the church was divided and fighting over certain externals, such as what they would eat and drink. Members took different positions and were judging or looking down with scorn on those who didn't agree with them. The apostle tried to bring them together in unity and told them that this was not what the kingdom was all about. He said in Romans 14:17: "For the kingdom of God is not a matter of eating and drinking, but of righteousness, peace and joy in the Holy Spirit."

Because the music of the kingdom is one of joy, be suspicious of religion that makes people angry, hostile, and judgmental.

Inclusiveness

God's kingdom is one that seeks everyone. Jesus once told a parable about a man who threw a banquet and invited all the right people, but many of them didn't come. At the end of the story He said in Luke 13:29, 30: "People will come from east and west and north and south, and will take their places at the feast in the kingdom of God. Indeed there are those who are last who will be first, and first who will be last."

Again, the divine kingdom turns things upside down. We tend to build walls to keep undesirables out. But God is in the business of tearing down walls, thus opening His kingdom to all who will enter, regardless of gender, race, ethnicity, or any other barrier that we might try to erect. We sing the music of the kingdom when we break down walls, bring people together, and overcome every vestige of prejudice.

Childlike Dependence

Finally, the music of God's kingdom is one of childlike dependence on Him. One day some mothers brought their children to Jesus to be blessed. Jesus' disciples were quite sure that their Master was far too busy to waste His time on little kids, so they tried to send them away. But Mark tells us that Jesus became angry at the disciples and told them, "Let the little children come to me, and do not hinder them, for the kingdom of God belongs to such as these. Truly I tell you, anyone who will not receive the kingdom of God like a little child will never enter it" (Mark 10:14, 15).

Probably we best hear the music of the kingdom in the voices of children. To sing the music of the kingdom is to become like children in total trust and dependence on God.

Summary

We can already sing the music of the kingdom in this world. In fact, it is by living the kingdom now that Christians give witness to what the kingdom is all about. And by singing the heavenly music now we draw others to enter it. The music of the kingdom has a distinctive sound. It is the music of heaven, already sung on earth in preparation for Christ's return. The themes of the music include:

Humility, not hubris
Service, not status
Generosity, not greed
Peace, not violence
Joy, not hostility
Open arms, not exclusion
Childlike dependence, not autonomy

God invites us to sing these melodies now. At first it may not seem that they are all that powerful in the world. After all, greed, power, force, and arrogance so often appear to win the day. But God says that His kingdom will ultimately triumph. Revelation 11:15 assures us that the day will come at Jesus' return when:

"The kingdom of the world has become the kingdom of our Lord and of his Messiah, and he will reign for ever and ever."

While the full manifestation of God's kingdom awaits Jesus' return, we can live in it until then. I like how N. T. Wright puts it at the end of his book *Simply Christian*. He emphasizes that God already opens the new world before us and invites us to follow Him into it.

"Made for spirituality, we wallow in introspection. Made for joy, we settle for pleasure. Made for justice, we clamor for vengeance. Made for relationship, we insist on our own way. Made for beauty, we are satisfied with sentiment. But new creation has already begun. The sun has begun to rise. Christians are called to leave behind, in the tomb of Jesus Christ, all that belongs to the brokenness and incompleteness of the present world. It is time, in the power of the Spirit, to take up our proper role, our fully human role, as agents, heralds, and stewards of the new day that is dawning. That, quite simply, is what it means to be Christian: to follow Jesus Christ into the new world, God's new world, which he has thrown open before us."[3]

One time Bernice Johnson Reagon, the founder of an a cappella singing group called Sweet Honey in the Rock, was asked how she was able to get people who attended the group's concerts to join them in singing the spirituals and gospel songs it performs with such vigor. She said that she tried to create a space that would allow the audience to be drawn into the singing, one that would persuade them that they had no choice but to sing. Then she said, "I think I make people feel that if they don't sing they are going to die."[4]

That sums it up pretty well. Unless we learn to sing the songs of the kingdom, we will die, for it is God's kingdom that will soon win the day when Jesus comes again. We can do more than be ready for that day—we can even now, in this world, live out in our lives what the kingdom is all about, and in doing so can draw others into the kingdom as well. "Even so, come, Lord Jesus" (Revelation 22:20, KJV).

---

[1] Quoted in William Paul Young, *The Shack* (Newbury Park, Calif.: Windblown Media, 2007), p. 250.

[2] N. T. Wright, *Simply Christian: Why Christianity Makes Sense* (New York: HarperCollins, 2006), p. 222.

[3] *Ibid.*, p. 237.

[4] Marva J. Dawn, *A Royal Waste of Time: The Splendor of Worshiping God and Being Church for the World* (Grand Rapids: Eerdmans, 1999), p. 341.

CHAPTER 14
LOOKING FORWARD TO THE DAY

One day as I was teaching a college class on the subject of the second coming of Christ, I decided to ask students if they had ever had dreams about it. I thought it would be a brief diversion before we continued with the rest of the agenda for the day. Was I ever wrong! We did nothing else that day but discuss the dreams that the class members had had. It was emotional and intense.

The first surprise was that so many of the students had dreamed about the Second Advent. The majority of them, in fact. The second, and more disturbing surprise, was that to a person all of their dreams were negative and scary. Not one had ever dreamed that they were delighted to be redeemed and would spend the rest of eternity with Jesus. Every single dream was about missing out on salvation. I will never forget some of the vivid examples my students shared.

One said he dreamed that he was standing, along with a whole group of people, on a railroad platform waiting for a train. The train pulled in, the conductor got off the train and started calling out the names of the would-be passengers, and one by one people boarded. As this process continued, the student recognized that the conductor was Jesus. The crowd on the platform got smaller and smaller as more and more got on the train, until finally he was the only one left. The conductor said, "All aboard," and started to enter the train. The student ran up to Him and said that he too should be on the list. The conductor said, "I'm sorry, but your name isn't here." Jesus boarded the train, then called "All aboard" once again, and the train took off with my student standing on the platform all alone. After it left the station, the train began rising into the air until it disappeared. The student remained on the platform, alone and crying. When he woke up, he really was crying.

Another student dreamed that he and his sister, along with their parents, were outside when they noticed a small cloud in the sky. Recognizing that it was the cloud that was bringing Jesus, they were all excited. As the cloud drew closer they could clearly see Jesus, and they shouted, "This is our God, and we have waited for Him." Then the cloud stopped overhead. Very slowly the student's mother, father, and sister began to rise from the ground. But the student stayed there. He tried to jump—to grab onto his family members. But nothing worked. Left behind, he had to watch as all of his family ascended with Christ.

Other students also recounted their dreams that day, and all were of the same character. Not a single one was happy and positive about the Second Coming.

This seems terribly unfortunate in light of the message of the New Testament about the Second Coming as good news that we have seen throughout this book. But it is hard for many to believe that the news is really that good. Yet Peter calls on Christians to look forward to the return of Christ, or as he calls it, the day of God. In 2 Peter 3 he talks about several aspects of the Second

Advent. He first speaks to the problem that we dealt with in chapter 4: the sense that God is being very slow about fulfilling His promise. Then He goes on to show certain ominous events associated with the Second Coming. He summons us to live holy lives in the light of what is approaching. But he concludes by admonishing us to look forward to the return of Jesus. The passage is long, but it is rich, so read it carefully.

"Above all, you must understand that in the last days scoffers will come, scoffing and following their own evil desires. They will say, 'Where is this "coming" he promised? Ever since our ancestors died, everything goes on as it has since the beginning of creation.' But they deliberately forget that long ago by God's word the heavens came into being and the earth was formed out of water and by water. By these waters also the world of that time was deluged and destroyed. By the same word the present heavens and earth are reserved for fire, being kept for the day of judgment and destruction of the ungodly. But do not forget this one thing, dear friends: With the Lord a day is like a thousand years, and a thousand years are like a day. The Lord is not slow in keeping his promise, as some understand slowness. Instead he is patient with you, not wanting anyone to perish, but everyone to come to repentance. But the day of the Lord will come like a thief. The heavens will disappear with a roar; the elements will be destroyed by fire, and the earth and everything done in it will be laid bare. Since everything will be destroyed in this way, what kind of people ought you to be? You ought to live holy and godly lives as you look forward to the day of God and speed its coming. That day will bring about the destruction of the heavens by fire, and the elements will melt in the heat. But in keeping with his promise we are looking forward to a new heaven and a new earth, where righteousness dwells" (2 Peter 3:3-13).

Peter says that we should not give up hope and think that because it has been so long the promise of the Second Advent will never come. God's timing is different from our own. This only reinforces what we have already seen in Acts 1:6-10 and Matthew 24:36. He then adds that the day will come as a thief. It will happen when people do not expect it. This again confirms what Jesus had said in Matthew 24. But Peter suggests a reason God seems to be taking so long. Compassionate and patient, He wants to save all those He can. He still has more children to include in His kingdom.

The apostle also admonishes us to be the kind of people we should be and to live the kind of lives that we should live in light of what awaits the world. We should exhibit holy and godly lives. He goes on in verse 14 of 2 Peter 3 to declare that we should be spotless, blameless, and at peace with God. Yet it should not scare us once we understand that it is God, through Christ, who makes us spotless and blameless. His grace saves us. God has taken the initiative to bring us into peace with Him. As we have seen before, we need trust only in His grace through Christ. Look at what Paul says in Romans 5:1: "Therefore, since we have been justified through faith, we have peace with God through our Lord Jesus Christ."

When we are justified by faith, we have peace

with God. Notice what the apostle adds about the basis for this peace we have with God in verses 6-10:

"You see, at just the right time, when we were still powerless, Christ died for the ungodly. Very rarely will anyone die for a righteous person, though for a good person someone might possibly dare to die. But God demonstrates his own love for us in this: While we were still sinners, Christ died for us. Since we have now been justified by his blood, how much more shall we be saved from God's wrath through him! For if, while we were God's enemies, we were reconciled to him through the death of his Son, how much more, having been reconciled, shall we be saved through his life!"

We don't need to worry about working our way to a godly life and finding peace with God. He has already taken care of that through Christ. We trust in Him and live for His kingdom. When we understand this, then the last part of Peter's teaching makes sense. He says we look forward to the Second Coming. In fact, he repeats it twice. I'm afraid that the dreams of my students testify that deep down we fear it more than look forward to it. But if, as we saw in chapter 2, it really is "this same Jesus" who is coming for us, that should hardly be true. We should be able to look forward to seeing One who saves us so freely and with such amazing grace and incredible love.

I have found some good news recently, however. I related the stories of my students' dreams in a sermon in the church where I now pastor and had several people tell me afterward that they had dreamed positive dreams about the Second Coming. Their dreams were not nightmares. They were excited in them and, finding themselves saved by His grace, they were caught up to meet Him in the air. That is good news. Maybe the message that the Second Coming is good news is getting out there and making a difference.

I hope this message of hope that we have seen in God's Word is good news for you, and that you can, with Peter, look forward to that day with eager expectation. That is what God invites us to do. When we celebrate the first advent of Christ to this world every Christmas, it is a time of joy. We feel the delight of Christmas as we remember the song of the angels above Bethlehem.

"But the angel said to them, 'Do not be afraid. I bring you good news that will cause great joy for all the people. Today in the town of David a Savior has been born to you'" (Luke 2:10, 11).

The anticipation of the Second Advent should also be a time of joy, for God has promised to make us ready for that day as we trust Him. Feel the gladness and sense of wonder in the following passage from Jude 24, 25:

"To him who is able to keep you from stumbling and to present you before his glorious presence without fault and with great joy—to the only God our Savior be glory, majesty, power and authority, through Jesus Christ our Lord, before all ages, now and forevermore! Amen."